*The text of this book is set in Caledonia
and the display in Bulmer.
Drawings are line ink.*

STEAMBOATS

A History of the Early Adventure

STEAMBOATS

A History of the Early Adventure

written and illustrated by RALPH T. WARD

THE BOBBS-MERRILL COMPANY, INC.

Indianapolis   New York

The Bobbs-Merrill Company, Inc.
Publishers   Indianapolis   New York
Copyright © 1973 by Ralph T. Ward
Design by Jack Jaget
Printed in the United States of America
All rights reserved
ISBN: 0-672-51785-X
Library of Congress catalog card number: 72-9888
0 9 8 7 6 5 4 3 2

ALLAN ROSS MACDOUGALL
Seaman & Journalist
1893–1956

Contents

Foreword

EUROPEANS, endlessly writing books about the young United States, often laughed and ridiculed Americans and their way of life. To them the young country was far too rough, too active, and much too democratic. They delighted, however, in recording that in one field, steamboating, Americans were well ahead of European efforts. The individual Americans who accomplished this are the subject of much of this book, from the wildly improbable beginning with John Fitch on the Delaware, to the rough-and-tumble conquest of the Mississippi by Nicholas J. Roosevelt and his wife, Lydia, and later the grand adventures of Henry Miller Shreve. The story—evolving from the hesitant development of the paddle wheel and steam engine to the time when freight carried on Mississippi steamboats was greater than that of England's maritime fleet traveling the oceans of the world—is a vital part of the history of America.

RTW

STEAMBOATS

A History of the Early Adventure

CHAPTER 1

Step One: Mechanical Boats Before Steam

IF YOU SAW the first steamboats ever built moving across the water, you might believe them to be spluttering mechanical toy rowboats or small excursion launches used to carry sightseers. You might even believe they were on fire, for they would be belching smoke and sparks and making a terrible racket as if they were about to blow up. Mixed with this odd assortment of unsafe-looking boats you would see two vessels of a fairly large size, the *Savannah* (1818) and the *Curaçao* (1825). You would notice immediately how small and unseaworthy they looked compared with present-day ships, and it is likely that you would hesitate to travel on such ships even for a short distance; yet the *Savannah* and the *Curaçao* were among the first vessels to cross the immense and dangerous Atlantic using steam for power. These first steamboats (and the larger steamships) were primitive vessels, and it took many years of research and experimentation to develop them. Their history is a fascinating one filled with adventure and drama.

Hundreds of years before steamboats became a reality various people attempted to create ships that moved by the use of mechanical gadgets instead of being propelled by the unreliable wind or by oars. The construction of such mechanical craft was considered a challenge even when the civilized world was confined to relatively small areas on the Mediterranean coast and in the Far East.

The first mechanical boats used paddle wheels operated by people or animals. In Rome, at the beginning of the First Punic War (264 B.C.), Appius Claudius Caudex led Roman troops beyond the Italian peninsula for the first time. A Roman sculptured relief shows the kind of ferry these troops used to cross the Strait of Messina to Sicily. The war vessels carrying the Roman legions

The first mechanical boats used paddle wheels operated by people or animals. From a medieval woodcut depicting the ships used by Appius Claudius Caudex in 264 B.C.

had three pairs of paddle wheels turned by two oxen at each set of wheels.

That such a mechanical boat could have been

successful is certain, for horse- or mule-powered boats, called teamboats, have been used all over the world at various times in history. The animals either walked on an upright circular treadmill or circled a shaft which was set in the hull and connected to the paddle wheels. Ferry boats used on the Mississippi River less than a hundred years ago looked very much like the craft used in 264 B.C.

During the years of Rome's decline, near the closing of the fourth century A.D., a memorandum, *On Matters of War*, written by an unknown author, suggested the use of oxen-operated paddle wheels on war ships. There are also a few references to ships operated by windmills in Roman history, but the case may well be that these vessels were actually floating mills used to grind grain, and not windmill-propelled craft. None of the mechanical vessels used in ancient Rome developed into permanent types of ships: they all seem to be isolated novelties.

Oriental peoples, too, developed an occasional mechanical vessel. In China a paddle boat operated by slaves working large circular treadmills was used over a thousand years ago. This vessel, and others like it built in the Orient, passed into history without creating much of a stir. The great maritime commerce of Asia has always been carried on by such efficient sailing craft as the junk and the sampan. Chinese naval history and tradition through the ages have been virtually static, for China, a landpower, has had little incentive to build a fighting navy or an aggressive merchant marine. Experimentation with mechanical boats, and even sailing craft, is almost nonexistent in Chinese history.

Although men and animals were used to power boats with paddle wheels again and again through the centuries, these primitive answers to the challenge of a mechanical craft were not satisfactory. Men and animals are not reliable as a source of power because they are easily exhausted. The only truly successful mechanical craft, such as galleys,

A medieval boat with paddle wheels.

were those in which oars have been used to move in and out of harbor when the wind was not favorable, or during war. In an emergency men could row large galleys for many miles in a day, but this did not often happen, for even the strongest rowers could not keep up such a pace for long.

During the Middle Ages hand-driven side wheels were used to propel small boats on rivers, and at times complicated variations were made in the arrangement of the paddles. These craft were probably nothing more than novelties, also, but during these years there was an increasing need for a paddle boat that worked. Rivers were being used more and more often than roads to transport goods. Cities were coming into existence all over the world in places they had not existed before, and industries were rapidly developing. As the population of the world grew, the demand for

During the Middle Ages hand-driven paddle wheels were used to propel small boats on rivers. These craft were probably nothing more than novelties.

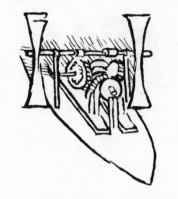

manufactured goods and food increased greatly, and in turn the need for reliable ships to carry such items developed.

In the 1400s Leonardo da Vinci, a brilliant inventor as well as a magnificent artist, probed the problem. In his scientifically advanced notebooks he wrote: ". . . make a large wheel of oars, and make a furrow from one end of the boat to the other where the wheel can touch the water." He also drew pictures of boats with paddle oars on both sides which were operated by a number of meshing gears. These boats were not practical,

In the 1400s Leonardo da Vinci probed the problem of paddle-driven vessels. In his notebooks he wrote: ". . . make a large wheel of oars, and make a furrow from one end of the boat to the other where the wheel can touch the water."

In 1511 the artist Raphael painted a picture of a boat pulled by two dolphins. A paddle wheel was also attached: how Raphael intended the wheel to help propel this whimsical craft is not known.

mainly because of the limited power available to move the paddles, for there were no advanced engines at the time.

In 1511 the artist Raphael painted a picture of a shell-shaped boat pulled by two dolphins. It has a paddle wheel attached to the side, but how he intended the wheel to help propel this whimsical craft is not known. The existence of this painting, however, and of the many other drawings depicting paddle devices, would indicate that the use of paddle wheels on boats was not so uncommon a practice as is sometimes believed.

In June of 1543 Blasco de Garvay, a Spanish naval officer, demonstrated a ship named the *Trinity* that moved by the use of two paddle wheels secreted in the hull; the ship was operated by fifty men. Emperor Charles V was supposed to be pres-ent when the ship was tested, but a member of his court dissuaded him from going. The visit was considered dangerous because a tank of boiling water, carried on deck for defense purposes, might have exploded. This tank was not connected with the movement of the paddle wheels in any way, but its presence on the ship has led some historians to claim (erroneously) that the *Trinity* was the first true steamship. Even if the records showed otherwise, this would be a far-fetched assertion, for during the 1500s the experiments dealing with steam in laboratories and alchemists' shops were all carried out on a primitive level. Surprisingly enough, however, in 1631—only eleven years after the Pilgrims landed at Plymouth Rock—a patent for what can be considered a "steam" boat was issued in England.

CHAPTER 2

Step Two: The Steam Engine

THE ATTEMPTS to use animals and humans to propel vessels were not very successful except over short routes, or within harbors by the use of horse-powered craft. What was needed to power mechanical vessels on long voyages was an engine that would move the ship along at a steady, regular clip: the steam engine was to be the first successful answer.

The steam engine is based on a simple principle. At sea level a quart of water heated to a temperature of 100° C. expands 1,849 times into 1,849 quarts of steam. In a partially closed system, the pressure produced by the expanding water turning to steam is employed to move parts of an engine, these parts turning a wheel or a gear or some other "working" part. The principle is simple, but to produce a steam engine that worked efficiently was a difficult engineering task. It took many years to go from the simple inventions of

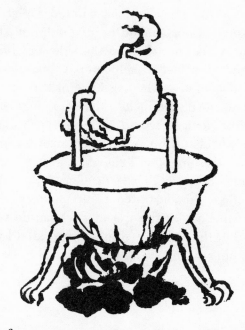

In the first century A.D., *Heron of Alexandria described a primitive steam turbine called a "aeolipile" which consisted of a hollow ball with two small outlet tubes. The ball was mounted on two brackets on the lid of a cauldron containing boiling water. One bracket was hollow and sent the steam into the ball, and as the steam escaped through the outlet tubes it turned the ball. This device, which showed the power of steam, was simply an experimental instrument.*

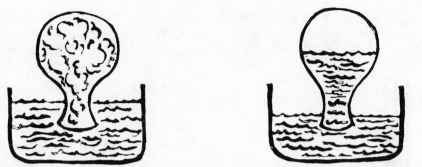

Giambattista della Porta's discovery: a steam-filled container turned upside down in a bowl of water. As the steam condenses, a partial vacuum is formed; atmospheric pressure then forces the water up into the container.

early scientists and engineers to the more complicated inventions of later experimenters.

The power of steam was known in ancient Egypt, but it was in Europe that the first steam devices of any practical use came into being. In Italy, where Galileo's startling discoveries in physics were astounding the world, another scientist, Giambattista della Porta, was writing a book on pneumatics, the study dealing with the mechanical properties of air and other gases. He described how the condensation of steam in a tightly closed vessel creates a partial vacuum. In della Porta's work, published in 1601, he mentions that he could demonstrate how a vacuum could be used to pull water up through a tube. But neither Galileo, who was interested in the experiment, nor della Porta really understood this simple pump. Like most scientists of that time, they believed that "nature abhors a vacuum," and since a vacuum could not occur in nature they concluded that the water was drawn upward to take the vacuum's place.

It was not until 1643 that the true nature of the steam pump, which is the basic idea behind all early apparatus using steam, was explained by Evangelista Torricelli, another Italian physicist. Torricelli studied the steam pump at Galileo's suggestion and decided that he was observing a simple mechanical effect: that air had weight

A simple mercury barometer, the sort used by Blaise Pascal to prove Evangelista Torricelli's theory concerning atmospheric pressure.

("atmospheric pressure"), and that this atmospheric pressure on the water pushed it upward through the tube. This theory was not acceptable to the scientific community at first; it went against the teachings of Aristotle who believed air had levity and tended to rise. But in 1646 the great French mathematician and physicist Blaise Pascal proved Torricelli was right by having his brother-in-law carry two barometers up the side of Puy-de-Dôme, a mountain near which Pascal had been born.

As the barometers were carried up the side of the mountain the columns of mercury within them dropped lower and lower. This occurred because the ocean of air above us is supported by whatever lies under it, solid or liquid. At sea level the pressure weighs against the barometer's opening, pushing the mercury upward in its enclosed tube. The farther up the mountain the barometer was carried the less the atmospheric pressure, therefore the mercury dropped.

In 1629 another inventive Italian, the architect Giovanni Branca, designed a machine utilizing the action of a jet of steam focused on the blades of a paddle wheel to produce rotary motion. Branca's machine may actually have been used to perform work in a mill in the town of Loretto. Also in the early 1600s Salomon de Caus, an engineer and architect who worked for Louis XIII, published a

Giovanni Branca's steam turbine.

book at Frankfort describing a simple machine to raise water by the use of a steam pump. Scientists, chemists, artists, engineers, and landscape architects experimented with the early steam pump: it was only a question of time before someone thought to put this pump to use for other purposes than drawing up water.

In England there are historical records about David Ramsey and Edward Ford, two mystery men so far as the steamboat's history is concerned.

In 1631 Ramsey was given a patent for an invention; it read, in part: "To raise water from low pitts by fire," and, "To make Boats, shippes and Barges to goe against strong Winde and Tyde." Ramsey's mystery is that today no one knows how he thought he could make a vessel go against the wind. A steam device was not mentioned in the patent, but it is probable that he intended to use a steam pump of some kind in all of the inventions covered by his patent: in those days such pumps were called "fire engines," and Ramsey's device operated by the use of a fire engine. Mr. Edward Ford is even more of a mystery. His patent, granted in 1640, is a vaguely described "schem" for moving ships against wind and tide "by some new great force." It sounds as if he had some idea of using a fire engine, but he kept the details of this "new great force" a secret.

Edward Somerset, second Marquis of Worcester, is often credited with the invention of the first practical "atmospheric steam engine." This claim is based on a pamphlet written in 1655 and published in 1663 which is oddly titled: *A Century of the Names and Scantlings* [patterns] *of Inventions by me Already Practiced.* The pamphlet contains a curious collection of descriptions of inventions that Somerset used. (Whether he invented them or not is a moot question.) One of these was a vague description of an apparatus for raising water by steam, supposedly operated near London. The description (there is no diagram) reads very much as if he had a simple water pump in mind, and not an engine at all.

There were many experiments with the "atmospheric pump," but the first breakthrough of sorts to the development of a workable engine came when Christian Huygens, a Dutch physicist and astronomer, mentioned an atmospheric machine with piston and cylinder in a memoir he wrote in 1680. Huygens was a scientist with a great reputation for his discoveries in astronomy such as the rings around Saturn, as well as for the invention of the pendulum clock which began progress toward accurate timekeeping.

Huygens's fame drew to him young physicists anxious to work under his guidance. One such

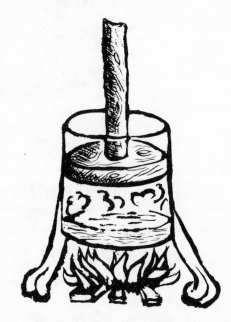

One of the earliest piston-and-cylinder devices, constructed by Denis Papin in 1690.

assistant was Denis (Dionysius) Papin who later invented the "steam digester," which we know as the pressure cooker. Papin, like many scientists in those days, traveled widely throughout Europe. At one time he assisted Robert Boyle, the Irish chemist who helped develop alchemy into the modern science of chemistry. Papin lived in many countries, finally settling in Germany, and it was there that his important experiments that contributed to the development of the steam engine were carried out. He suggested that the condensation of steam could be employed to make a vacuum under a piston which had been raised by the expansion of the steam itself. (Huygens had already worked on a similar device using gunpowder to raise the piston.) When Papin put his theory to work in 1690, he constructed the earliest cylinder-and-piston device using steam.

Papin's device did not work, however, for he used the same container for both boiler and cylinder. Nonetheless, Papin believed that one day an effective engine would be built along these lines. He even suggested that it might be used to propel boats. Later, in 1707, he did build a paddle boat, but manual power was used to operate it. He was one of the many scientists of the day interested in mechanical vessels.

In 1689 Thomas Savery in England developed

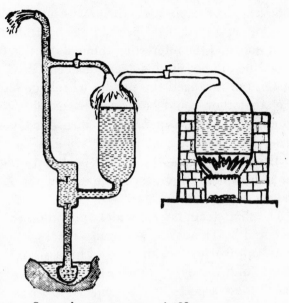

Thomas Savery's steam pump of 1689.

the earliest practical steam apparatus. It was a simple steam pump, but dangerous and not very efficient. By taking Savery's pump and adding the safety valve Papin had invented for his pressure cooker, John Theophilus Desaguliers developed a much safer pumping system. Desaguliers, who was born in France in 1688, was a man of many interests; besides his work in theoretical mechanics and optics, he did much to popularize electrical science.

Savery, like Papin and others, was interested in developing a boat that operated mechanically. He built one, and the interesting thing about this boat is that he did not use his steam device to drive the vessel, but arranged the paddle wheels in such a way that they could be moved by using a rope-winding apparatus operated by men. He spent a good deal of time and money trying to get the British Navy to adopt his paddle boat and went so far as to exhibit it on the Thames, but the Navy showed no interest.

The first steam engine widely put into use was invented by Thomas Newcomen, a blacksmith and metal craftsman, with the help of his assistant and friend John Calley, a plumber and glazier. One of the saddest aspects of Newcomen's life was that many members of the scientific societies of his day refused to take his experiments seriously. A few did, but most believed that a man of his background could not add anything of importance to human knowledge. They were forgetting the example of that great Dutch microscopist Anton van Leeuwenhoek, who was living and working at the same time, and who discovered protozoa and bacteria. Van Leeuwenhoek, who was honored by many scientific societies, not only ran a dry goods store, but was the janitor at the Delft City Hall.

Newcomen, from the details available, seems to have led a peaceful, happy life, working in near obscurity for years to develop the first *true* engine: a machine that harnesses heat energy to produce force and motion. His first successful engine, built in 1705, was a very small one. It used an internal condensing jet; that is, a squirt of cold water was sent into the steam-filled cylinder condensing the steam back into water. This jet of water caused a vacuum to be created in the cylinder. Atmospheric pressure then forced the piston downward, and when steam was again introduced into the cylinder the piston rose. Even after Newcomen proved that his steam engine worked he could not sell one for many years. The first, aside from his own small model, was built in 1712. It was housed in an enormous brick building and was so large and unwieldy that you might not think of it as an engine at all. Before Thomas Newcomen died in 1729 his engines were used in Austria, France, England, and elsewhere.

Many other men experimented with steam engines in the early eighteenth century, but Newcomen's work is of special importance, not only because it was the first true engine, but because, later in the century, it was so widely accepted. Newcomen's engines, employed at the waterworks of many cities to pump water, were popular places to visit. They became tourist curiosities for young

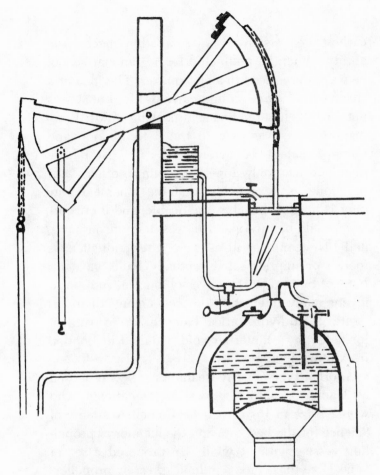

A simplified version of the first true engine: a device that harnesses heat energy to produce force and motion. The first steam engine, pictured above, was constructed by Thomas Newcomen in England in the 1700s.

and old alike: people were not so afraid, as they formerly had been, of steam under pressure. Seeing Newcomen's engines work so well, people in business, science, and education took an interest in the power of steam, and the improvement of the steam engine was almost assured.

It was not long before Newcomen's engine was considered as a source of power in a mechanical boat. In 1729 in England, a Dr. John Allen patented a steamboat with a Newcomen engine. This vessel worked on the principle of water jet propulsion, always a popular approach in Europe. Then, on December 21, 1736, Jonathan Hulls, encouraged by a wealthy patron, one Mr. Freeman, took out a patent for a "steamboat." The next year Hulls published a pamphlet describing the types of ships he had in mind in which a Newcomen engine could be used. It was titled: *A Description and Draft* [drawing] *of a new-invented Machine for Carrying Vessels or Ships out of or into any Harbour, Port, or River against Wind and Tyde, or in a Calm.*

It is seldom noted that Hulls's proposal concerned four types of steam vessels, and that these four types of steam-powered vessels were the forerunners of all later steamboat experiments. Most researchers assume that the vessel illustrated in the pamphlet, a stern-wheeled tug towing a large

One of the four steamboats designed by the brilliant Jonathan Hulls. Hulls wrote in 1736: ". . . if what I have imagined may only appear as plain to others as it has done to me, that the scheme I now offer [the steamboat] is practicable, and if encouraged, will be useful."

three-masted ship, was the only steam craft invented by the brilliant Hulls. Actually, Hulls suggested three other vessels: a steamboat propelled by poles—a type that James Rumsey of Virginia later experimented with in America; a vessel with a portable engine—a feature common to most small craft today; and a third type of steamboat—one that used paddle wheels on both sides of the boat. The steam vessel with side paddle wheels was the type eventually adopted by most of the successful early steamboat experimenters.

Hulls was born in England in 1699, and from his earliest years showed a remarkable mechanical ability. When he graduated from grammar school he was apprenticed to a clockmaker. The idea of a steam vessel came to him early in life, but it was not until he had the financial backing of Mr. Freeman that he was able to travel to London and obtain a patent. He wrote: ". . . if what I have imagined may only appear as plain to others as it has done to me, namely, that the scheme I now offer [the steamboat] is practicable, and if encouraged, will be useful." He was not encouraged, and his steamboat ideas were often ridiculed as foolish or impractical. Eventually Hulls gave up hope of building a steam vessel, but he went on to invent many interesting devices, among them his "statical and hydrostatical balance," an instrument for detecting counterfeit gold. He died in London in extreme poverty.

Another type of early steam vessel was proposed by Daniel Bernouilli, a Swiss mathematician, who won a prize in 1750 from the French Academy of Science for the best essay on the manner of propelling vessels without wind. He proposed a set of vanes, like those on a windmill (a screw propeller, in fact), driven by either animal or steam power. Also at this time Abbé Gautier in France suggested using the Newcomen engine to drive side paddle wheels. In Scotland someone proposed propelling ships by using a primitive form of jet propulsion: a cannon fired from the stern. These men's ideas show how wide the interest in mechanical navigation was during the eighteenth century.

But improvements were needed in the Newcomen engine before one could satisfactorily power a vessel. The first great change came when John Smeaton, an engineer, took out a patent in 1769 for an improved Newcomen engine. Smeaton used better proportions when building his engine and was able to increase the speed of the piston.

It was, however, James Watt, a Scotsman with an inquiring mind as well as patience and determination, whose contributions changed the form of the steam engine and whose improvements assured its final acceptance and wide use. As a boy Watt showed outstanding capabilities, especially in the study of mathematics. He lived in a small seaport town. In order to improve his chances of getting the best education as a mathematical instrument maker, he went to Glasgow in 1754 when he was eighteen.

His teacher at Glasgow made an enormous error in judgment; he thought young Watt slow and stupid, in fact incapable of learning much of anything. Watt, however, had faith in himself, so he went to London and began an apprenticeship with another instrument maker. Because of poor health he was not able to complete his years of study. Returning to Glasgow he set up his own shop and was appointed to the post of "mathematical instrument maker" at the University of Glasgow.

At this time Joseph Black became a close friend of his. Black was the discoverer of latent heat, the heat that changes water to steam. The same amount of heat that is required to change a quart of water into 1,849 quarts of steam is released when that steam condenses back into water (if the temperature and pressure are kept constant).

With Black and other friends, Watt often passed his time talking about how to improve the steam engine. The discussions were stimulating to the young men, and on a high scientific level. The student who had been thought to be "incapable of learning" was discussing problems in advanced pneumatics with some of the greatest men of the age. Watt was certain that there was a way of making Newcomen's engine work more efficiently, but he and his friends dealt in theory, that is, something yet to be proven.

In 1763 or 1764—no one is certain which—Watt was asked to fix a model of a Newcomen engine that was in the university's collection of scientific devices. The model did not work really well even after Watt repaired it, and he felt certain he could build a better engine: now was the time to put to the test the theories he and his friends had often discussed. He began a long series of experiments which resulted in a greatly improved steam engine.

What had especially interested Watt about the model was that he could not get it to work for more than a few strokes: he therefore concluded that it was a very inefficient engine. Actually, the fault was with the model and not Newcomen's engine. The model exaggerated the engine's inefficiency because heat loss, plus losses due to friction, increases as size diminishes, and the model was a small one.

The experiments Watt undertook concerning the Newcomen engine were not easy to do. Sometimes they were with the engine itself, but often they were simply with scientific equipment in his instrument shop. His experiments dealt with the relation of the density and pressure of steam to its temperature, and he concluded that the temperature of the steam should be as low as possible when used to create a vacuum. He also discovered, as he wrote, that "the cylinder should be always as hot as the steam which entered it." But the crucial question was: How could he apply his discoveries to Newcomen's engine?

The answer came to Watt not while he was in his workshop, but as he took a walk one May day in 1765. It suddenly occurred to him that the steam should be condensed in a container separate from the cylinder, forced into this condenser by the downward stroke of the piston. By the time he had finished his stroll the complete concept of the new steam engine was arranged in his mind. He put these ideas into working engines and found the increased efficiency astounding.

But it was not until four long years later that Watt was able to take out his first patent since it took that long to build a reliable engine. By 1774, with continued improvement, Watt had changed Newcomen's "atmospheric engine" to the Watt steam engine complete in all essential details. Still, for ten long years, from 1775 until 1785, Watt continued to experiment and improve his engine, and during that time he took out five new patents. When, with a business partner, he began building his engines they proved an exceptional success, and the demand was tremendous.

James Watt, the "slow" student, was honored in his country, and in others. When he died in 1819 the English provided a tomb for him in Westminster Abbey. English industry had profited enormously from this Scotsman's great work. The epitaph on his tomb reads, in part: ". . . *JAMES WATT*, who, directing the force of an original genius, early exercised in philosophic research, to the improvement of *THE STEAM ENGINE . . ."*

In the history of ships, efficient engines meant that new types of vessels could be built: the age of rapid transportation at sea was about to begin with the introduction of the first practical steamboats.

A simplified version of the Watt engine.

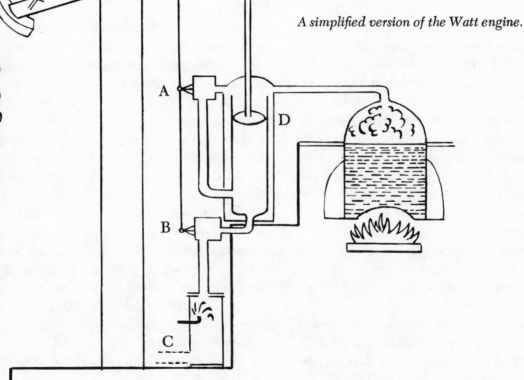

CHAPTER 3

The Early Successful Adventures in France and America

IF SOMEONE asked you to guess at the occupations of the earliest inventors of steamboats, you might head the list with engineer, naval architect, or perhaps a seaman of one kind or another; it is not likely that you would include two innkeepers, two French noblemen, a silversmith, and a clockmaker. Yet these were the occupations of the men who led the way in building the earliest working steamboats.

Comte Joseph d'Auxiron, a French army officer, was one of the first experimenters in Europe. He built a stern paddle boat to be propelled by a Newcomen engine. It mysteriously sank just prior to its trial on the river Seine in 1774. He died before the boat was recovered and the experiment was abandoned.

Almost ten years later, on July 15, 1783, crowds of people along the Saône River watched in amazement as a steam-powered boat designed by

Marquis Claude de Jouffroy d'Abbans worked its way upriver for fifteen minutes. Excited local scientists among the crowd who observed the world's first successful steamboat—a side paddle wheeler—run its short course excitedly wrote up a report of the event.

Through the ages the French have shown maritime genius in designing ships. The outstanding intelligence the French shipbuilders used in designing men-of-war is part of the glory of French history. In the American War of Independence (1776–83) the victory of the original thirteen states over the English at Yorktown would not have been possible without the help of French ships and men. While the war raged in America, Jouffroy, working quietly in France, began to discover the answer to the centuries-old puzzle of an engine-powered vessel.

Jouffroy's story concerning the steamboat be-

The Pyroscaphe *based on a drawing by Marthe de Jouffroy
in the Besançon Municipal Library.*

gan in his youth when he was exiled to Provence from Paris for dueling. He spent some time in a prison because of this incident, but jail was not always a real hardship in those days—if you were a nobleman. His cell would probably be fairly large, something like a one-room apartment. With money he could buy books, ink, pen and paper, set up a desk and spend hours reading and writing. He would have sufficient food cooked to his taste if he could afford it and even keep a servant to tidy up the cell and run errands. Marco Polo wrote his book about his journey to the Orient while he was in jail; Sir Walter Raleigh wrote his history of the world while being held a prisoner; and Jouffroy studied ornithology and also wrote a book about ships while in prison on the Island of Sainte-Marguerite.

When he returned to Paris at the age of twenty-four in 1775, steamboat building was coming more into vogue. That year Jacques C. Périer managed to move a small boat by steam power on the Seine. It was not a very successful trial. Jouffroy thought he could do better, and he sought out influential men to help back his project. The majority of potential backers did not think his approach "scientific" because Jouffroy insisted that a powerful engine was required.

The idea of a powerful engine was the opposite of Périer's, and Périer was respected as the most knowledgeable man in France concerning engines and steamboats. Périer believed that the less power used on a boat the more successful it would prove, for he thought less power was needed to drive a boat on water than a vehicle on land. His idea was to use a one-horse-power engine. Jouffroy calculated that a powerful engine was required. Convinced that Périer was wrong, young Jouffroy left Paris and went home to begin work on the problem.

His first boat was a small one propelled with web-footed paddles; it did not work. Then he decided to build a large boat, about a hundred and fifty feet long and fourteen feet wide. The larger boat was called for because Jouffroy intended to use a more powerful engine than the engine used in his first attempt. He named the boat *Pyroscaphe* (fire boat). In the early days of steamboating steam vessels were often called fire boats because of the "fire engine" used aboard them and the fires roaring in the boilers and the clouds of smoke and burning sparks which they produced.

Jouffroy's engine was a Newcomen type; instead of web-footed paddles for his second craft he used paddle wheels at both sides. All the important features of the steamboat for years to come were included in Jouffroy's *Pyroscaphe*.

The trial of the large boat took place on June 15, 1783, on the Saône River near Lyons: it was successful and the crowds cheered, but the event was greatly overshadowed by two other experiments in transportation that took place in France the same year. On June 5, 1783, Joseph and Étienne Montgolfier filled a balloon with heated air that rose to a height of sixteen hundred feet—and this event took place not far from Lyons. This was the beginning of flight, as people thought of it at the time, and the balloon flew for an incredible length of time—ten minutes. The first balloon passengers were a duck, a sheep, and a rooster.

Then, on August 27 that same year a hydrogen-filled balloon designed by Jacques-Alexandre Charles made an ascent from Paris before almost half the excited population of that city who were anxious to be present at the birth of the age of air travel. When the hydrogen-filled balloon landed fifteen miles away a crowd of villagers, unaware of the origin of the flying craft, tore it to pieces. They thought it was an unidentified flying object sent with hostile intentions by invaders.

Unfortunately for Jouffroy, 1783 was the year that the balloon craze began. Compared to flight in the sky, steamboating seemed ordinary. Many men experimenting with steam navigation were to bemoan the fact that money could be had for balloon building, but hardly any was available for steamboat construction.

Although the trial of the *Pyroscaphe* was over-

Compared to flying, steamboating seemed ordinary. Men experimenting with steam navigation resented the fact that money was easily available for balloon building but not for steamboat construction. Left, the first Montgolfier balloon was a simple bag filled with heated air and smoke. Below, the first balloon passengers: a duck, a sheep and a rooster.

shadowed by the balloon events, the members of the scientific academy of Lyons signed an affidavit saying the boat had moved up the river for fifteen minutes. Jouffroy sent this affidavit to Paris to secure a monopoly on steamboat construction. The government had promised the exclusive right to build and operate steamboats in France to the first man who successfully ran one that was practical. Jouffroy never received this right, for the government officials asked the Academy of Sciences in Paris to approve Jouffroy's affidavit. The members in Paris, led by Périer, Jouffroy's competitor, failed to approve Jouffroy's claim.

They argued that Jouffroy was not capable of accomplishing such a great feat, for after all, he

was only a petty nobleman from the backwoods: he was not a "scientist." They reasoned that if Périer had not been successful, how was it possible for Jouffroy to succeed? Since there was, however, a slight chance that he had actually built a workable boat, they recommended that he come to Paris and show them that he could repeat the experiment. But there was a catch even to this offer: they required that for the new trial Jouffroy's boat must travel many miles up the Seine and carry 300 metric tons, or nearly 700,000 pounds.

Jouffroy was stunned by the request. The *Pyroscaphe* had been successful at the trial, but it was almost totally destroyed during its first short run.

For the new trial in Paris a new boat would have to be built. Besides, to build a boat that could carry such a burden was a near impossibility, especially since the powerful Watt engines were not being exported from England and he would have to use the less efficient Newcomen type. Even with a Watt engine it is doubtful, at this stage, if Jouffroy could have complied with the conditions unless he spent great sums of money and many years working on the project.

There were other pressures on Jouffroy that did not favor his continuing with his experiments. He was severely ridiculed by his family and friends who thought his work with engines degrading, something done only by common men of low birth. When he went to the royal court he was openly laughed at for the same reason, and for the fact that he expressed ideas in opposition to such men as Périer. When such conditions are taken into consideration we realize that Jouffroy must have had a passionate drive to build steamboats in the first place.

He had spent nearly ten years and much of his own fortune on his steamboats, but now without help, without encouragement, without the acknowledgment of his great achievement from his countrymen, the Marquis Claude de Jouffroy d'Abbans gave up his dream. The French Revolu-tion (1789–99) soon made him an exile for a second time. On his return to France some years later, he did manage to set up a steamboat company and to build and operate a steam vessel on the Seine; but by that time Robert Fulton and Robert Livingston had sailed their steamboat up the Hudson, and Fulton was given the credit for the invention.

The next steamboat, and the first really successful working one, was built in the United States shortly after the War of Independence. Its name was the *Experiment,* and it carried many eager and delighted passengers up and down the Delaware River during the summer of 1790. John Fitch designed this boat and put it together with the help of Henry Voight, who worked with Fitch on the engine.

The *Experiment* was a good name for the craft, for it was only one of many steamboats that Fitch designed. It is not so easy as it may seem to power a boat with an engine, especially if you have no models to go by. Fitch wrote: "I know of nothing so perplexing and vexatious to a man of feeling as . . . steamboat building." There was good reason for these words, for many men were defeated and ruined in trying to develop the steamboat.

John Fitch was born in Windsor, Connecticut, in 1743. By the time he began his steamboat

The Pyroscaphe *based on a model in Paris. Although Marthe de Jouffroy's drawing is perhaps more accurate,*
this model is considered a likely representation of Jouffroy's successful steamer.

experiments he had already had a career as a land developer. In 1785 Fitch thought of using a steam engine to propel a wagon on land. It was an inspiration which seemed faultless until he considered the condition of the roads in the young United States.

Most of the roads were simple trails and people walked or used horseback. Daniel Webster made the trip from New Hampshire to Massachusetts in 1796 by horseback, for as he wrote later, stage-coaches ". . . no more ran into the center of New Hampshire than they ran to Baffins Bay." In 1775 it took George Washington twelve days to go from Philadelphia to Boston to take command of the

A stagecoach in the late 1700s.

Continental Army, and this was considered good time.

In 1797 a writer in the *American Annual Register* said: "The roads from Philadelphia to Baltimore exhibit, for the greater part of the way, an aspect of savage desolation." Besides, the roads were dangerous, for if coaches were used they often overturned and passengers were injured and sometimes killed. In winter, travel came to a standstill for weeks at a time. Wheeled vehicles were not common—in Boston in 1798 there were only 145 privately owned wheeled vehicles. Even horses were generally only used near settlements or on beaten paths. Most travelers on long journeys through inland areas went on foot most of the way, and progress through wooded areas, which meant practically all of the known country, was by Indian trails that were often "obstructed by fallen trees, old logs, miry places, pointed rocks and entangling roots," as Gideon Hawley recorded in 1753.

There were, however, many navigable rivers and streams, and they provided one of the main means of getting from settlement to settlement. The use of large and small sailing craft was common on rivers such as the Hudson, Delaware, and Connecticut, and in areas such as Chesapeake Bay. Small boats were used by families who lived on the coast, or near bays or rivers, much as an automobile is used today. This was the situation that faced John Fitch in 1785, and it is no wonder that he quickly gave up the idea of a land vehicle powered by steam and decided to build a vehicle for travel on water.

How John Fitch accomplished the great achievement of building and running the first practical steamboat is a curious story, especially since he was not an engineer and knew nothing about steam engines when he began his experiments. Fitch had been a prosperous silversmith until the War of Independence began; then he joined the army. In those days enlistments were often for brief periods, and men joined and left the army pretty much at will, so after a short stint Fitch decided to open a gun repair shop.

When the English destroyed Fitch's workshop he decided to try his hand at supplying Washington's troops with such items as tobacco and blankets during their bitter and disheartening winter at Valley Forge. He earned a great deal of money selling supplies to the army, but the money was colonial currency and virtually worthless. He invested in lands in Kentucky, but while surveying them he was captured by Indians and after many terrifying experiences he made his way back East. Unable to find a place for himself in the post-war world of the young United States, Fitch, already in his forties, returned to the wilderness.

He said in his autobiography, the source for most of the material concerning his life, that he had not known there was such a thing as a steam engine when the idea of a steam-powered vehicle came to him. When he was shown a description of a Newcomen engine he was amazed. As for the more advanced Watt engines, few people in America even knew of their existence. The first experimental steam engine in the U.S. was of the Newcomen type, and it was not built until 1773. There were only three large, working engines in the whole country, but this did not deter Fitch. Even if you do not trust John Fitch's word about his ignorance concerning the steam engine, his task was still a formidable one, for he had to scale

down a Newcomen engine (most of them were huge) to such a degree that it was like inventing a new engine altogether.

Fitch made a model that illustrated his idea of a steamboat. The model is perhaps significant, pointing up his lack of engineering skill at this point in his life: the only indication of a steam engine is a smoke stack. He showed the model to Dr. John Ewing, the Provost of the University of Pennsylvania, and Ewing wrote: "I have examined Mr. Fitch's machine . . . It is certain that the extensive force of water, when converted into

The model of John Fitch's steamboat.

steam, is equal to any obstruction that can be laid in its way." He praises steam, but does not seem heartily to endorse Fitch's boat. Fitch, however, was so pleased with this endorsement that he decided to put his idea before Congress in New York City, the early capital. As he traveled there he showed his model and Ewing's letter to other important men, and others endorsed the idea also. Elated by their further encouragement, Fitch was certain Congress would congratulate him and, most important, offer financial assistance. Fitch was a poor man and needed money more than anything else to foster his steamboat plan.

He submitted his proposal to Congress on August 29, 1785. It was sent to a committee of three members and rejected. So far as any records show they made no report on Fitch's "machine" which was, as Fitch wrote, to "facilitate the internal Navigation of the United States, adapted especially to the Waters of the Mississippi." Perhaps the committee did make a report, and perhaps they pointed out that the Mississippi River was under Spanish control. (It had been French territory until 1762, given to Spain until 1800 when by secret treaty it was returned to France. Not until 1803 did the U.S. purchase the Louisiana Territory from France, and this opened the Mississippi to travel by Americans.) In any case, at that point in the history of the United States, minutes of Congress were general and vague, confined to very important matters conducted by the new nation, and the committee report might easily not have been included.

Fitch decided to build a steamboat anyway, partly to demonstrate to the Congressmen how mistaken they had been in rejecting his proposal. He was penniless and had to plead for money everywhere. He tried to gain the support of Benjamin Franklin. This would have made his fund raising easier, but although Franklin spoke pleasantly to Fitch, his interests in steam navigation had been influenced by his years in Europe: Franklin thought a "pump boat" (jet propulsion by water) with a "fire engine" was the answer. Besides, Franklin was backing another American, James Rumsey of Virginia, who was working on just such a "pump boat" at the time; so pleasant talk was all Fitch got from Franklin.

Next Fitch went to Thomas Johnson, the former governor of Maryland. Johnson was impressed and suggested that Fitch speak to General Washington. But, Washington was also backing Rumsey's boat which was to use a jet of water exhausted at the stern to move it forward, so, after a rather unnerving and disjointed conversation with Washington, Fitch was turned away. Although all these great men thought the personable Rumsey was the more likely to succeed, he never produced a practical working boat.

One of the men Fitch visited during these travels was William Henry of Lancaster, Pennsylvania. Henry mentioned that he had, years before, thought of building a steamboat: he showed the unbelieving Fitch the drawings he had made for the boat. Henry was a very busy man, but he liked the idea of Fitch's having gone before Congress with the plan of a steamboat—it was what the country needed. Generously he offered to make Fitch a model of an engine, which he did, and which Fitch greatly appreciated. Henry wished Fitch luck, although he was pessimistic. Three years earlier he had said: "I am doubtful whether such a machine will find favor with the public, as everyone considers it impractical . . ." But now Fitch had the model of his steamboat with its paddle belt, an endless chain with paddles, and he also had a fair idea of how a steam engine worked.

Fitch did not give up hope in spite of finding no financial support for his scheme. He traveled from state to state begging the various assemblies and legislatures for encouragement in the form of financial assistance: they all refused. He spoke to such men as Patrick Henry and James Madison, and a long roster of others then famous in

John Fitch's steamboat of 1786.

America. Then, he changed his tactics: instead of asking for money he petitioned the state of New Jersey for the exclusive right to navigate the waters of that state by steam. On March 18, 1786, they granted him that right. The legislators had not been willing to part with a penny, but they readily voted to bestow a favor.

The tide had turned for Fitch; within weeks he had, on the strength of the New Jersey grant, organized a steamboat company. The money to build a small craft at last was made available by people who bought shares in his company. Now the problem was to get a steam engine. Fitch turned to one of those mechanical jack-of-all-trades of those times, a clockmaker, Henry Voight. Together Fitch and Voight built a primitive steam engine, put it into a light, open boat called a skiff and added paddles arranged six to a side which worked by means of cranks connected to the engine.

They tried this steamboat out in the summer of 1786—and it worked. Eagerly Fitch reported the success to the members of the company, asking for more money to build a larger craft. Some of the shareholders had lost interest in the enterprise, others could not face the ridicule of supporting a "mad man," so they voted "no" to more funds.

At this point many people would have said: "So much for that," and gone on to something else. But the steamboat had become an obsession with Fitch. He believed he could build one that would run on a regular schedule and carry hundreds of passengers. He wrote the Pennsylvania Assembly asking for a loan, saying: "There is such a strange infatuation in mankind that it seems they would rather lay out there [their—spelling, punctuation, and the use of capitals were not regulated to any great degree until the next century] money in Bellons [balloons] and Fireworks, and be a pest to Society than to lay it out in something that would be of use to themselves and Country." Although he was right, the legislature refused the loan. Perhaps the politicians were annoyed that Fitch lectured to them, more likely they simply did not want to part with any money for a doubtful scheme.

The same Assembly was willing enough, however, when Fitch applied for a monopoly of steam navigation the next year, to vote in his favor. Delaware and Virginia also granted Fitch similar monopolies. The idea of such monopolies is ancient. The word itself translated from the ancient Greek roughly equals a "single seller of a product," or one person given the right to sell a specific item. In France, Spain, and elsewhere the king granted such monopolies to the sellers of cloth and other items. Monopolies were the earliest form of issuing a patent on an invention. In 1789 John Stevens, who will be discussed later, petitioned Congress for patents to cover a boiler, and it was due to this petition that legislation was passed in April 1790 framing the first patent law of the United States. But there was no patent office until 1802; before that, and even after, monopolies were granted in particular fields covering the use of machinery—Fitch's "machine" was the steamboat.

On the strength of these new monopolies granted in 1787 Fitch reorganized his company; investors were impressed by the possibility of growth and profit. Fitch had money again and set about building a larger boat. The hulls, or the main bodies, of each of these early steamboats were built by professional boatbuilders. Fitch did not actually start from the keel up; his boats were delivered to him, then by adding paddles and power he turned them into steamboats.

With Voight's help the engine was greatly improved, and in August of 1787 the trials proved very successful. Judge Ellsworth, a member of the Federal Convention, "was on board the boat," as he said, "and saw the experiment succeed." David Rittenhouse, an engineer and scientist, said that he had "Frequently seen Mr. Fitch's steamboat, which, with great labour and perseverance, he has at length compleated." Rittenhouse went on board and marveled that the ship worked so easily. He was also impressed by its speed: three miles an hour. Fitch was *not* impressed: he hoped eventually to produce a steam vessel that would go from ten to fourteen miles an hour.

These were the years of success for Fitch, but they were also the beginning of the long years of difficult destitution: during the rest of his life he was always chronically in need of money. Fitch's company bought a sixty-foot-long hull that he christened the *Experiment*. Then he and Voight worked on the engine until it seemed perfect. Fitch put four large, broad paddles at the stern which were operated by a series of gears and chain belts. In July of 1788 the first extensive trial took place.

It went off almost without a hitch. The boat easily traveled up the Delaware from Philadelphia to Burlington, New Jersey. It had almost reached the Burlington pier when the boiler developed a leak and the engine went dead. The people on the boats they had passed with ease going up the river hooted and laughed as the *Experiment* was forced to drop helplessly down the river. The people who joked and ridiculed Fitch and his backers did not realize that at the time this was the longest and most successful steamboat trip ever made. When the boiler was repaired, the boat made several round trips to Burlington. On October 12, 1788, the steamboat carried thirty passengers. For the next year and a half Fitch, living the poorest life, improved the boat's performance and finally managed to produce the first workaday steamboat.

On June 14, 1790, an advertisement ran in a number of Pennsylvania newspapers, which read: "THE STEAMBOAT is now ready to take passengers, and is intended to set off from Arch Street Ferry, in Philadelphia, every Monday, Wednesday, and Friday, for Burlington, Bristol, Bordertown, & Trenton, to return on Tuesdays, Thursdays and Saturdays."

The boat ran from June to September. It was used on Sundays as an excursion boat, and it was popular and successful. One reader wrote to the *New York Magazine* that: "Fitch's steamboat

John Fitch's Experiment, *depicted in early prints with three paddles, whereas it actually had four.*
It began operation in July of 1788 and was put into commercial use in June of 1790.

really performs to a charm. It is a pleasure, while one is on board of her in a contrary wind, to observe her superiority over the river shallops, sloops, ships, etc., who, to gain anything, must make a zigzag course, while this, our new invented vessel, proceeds in a direct line. . . Fitch is certainly one of the most ingenious creatures alive, and will certainly make his fortune . . ."

It was not to be the case, however. The operation of the steamboat cost the company more money than the fares produced. The backers, mostly small merchants such as grocers, discouraged by the lack of profit, were again losing interest, but Fitch went forward and began building a more powerful and larger boat, aptly called the *Perseverance*. It was not completed in time to meet the specifications of the monopolies, and when he lost these his backers abandoned him.

Ridiculed, and without money, Fitch continued to try to interest people in steamboat navigation. People turned their backs on him even after he had shown that the steamboat would work month after month. He tried to interest the Spanish government in the idea of using steamboats on the Mississippi, but they rejected his proposal. He went to France believing he would find help there, but when he arrived he found life disordered due to the French Revolution. He stayed with Aaron Vail, who owned the European rights to his steamboat, but waiting for the disorders to end Fitch grew impatient and went to England to see if he could buy a Boulton and Watt engine. Finding the government forbade its export he returned home.

Finally, disheartened and poverty-stricken, he went back into the wilderness of Kentucky, where at fifty-five John Fitch, the builder of the first successfully operated steamboat, died in 1798. He had been right about the future of steam, and soon the Mississippi teemed with steamboats and the Atlantic was crossed. He was right, also, when he said to a friend: "I shall not live to see the time, you will, when steamboats will be preferred to all other means of conveyance . . ." Others were to achieve fame and fortune working in the same field that he had experimented in so heroically, fighting against great odds and humiliating jeers. But the first battle had been won by Fitch.

CHAPTER 4

Steamboat's A-Coming!

DURING the early 1800s the world went "steamboat crazy." Travelers began describing trips on steamboats, as one German woman novelist did, as "flying upon wings of steam." The cry "Steamboat's a-coming!" was heard at coastal and inland harbors: it was a shout of happiness, for the steamboat brought news of the outside world, mail from distant places, friends and relatives returning home or to visit; it also brought new settlers and merchandise from manufacturing centers and far-off lands. When the first steamboat was built in Maine, Lewis Pease, a local poet, commemorated this happy and important occasion by writing:

> A fig for all your clumsy craft,
> Your pleasure boats and packets;
> The steamboat lands you safe and soon
> At Mansfield's, Trott's or Brackets'.

The jeers that had taunted John Fitch turned to cheers for such men as John Stevens, Robert Fulton, and Henry Bell. This change of attitude occurred for a number of reasons; a prime reason was the improvement in the boats themselves. The early Hudson and Mississippi steamboats were not simple excursion day-boats as Fitch's had been; they were somewhat like floating hotels, serving meals and supplying sleeping accommodations which were included in the price of the passage. Also, the great difference between the price of stage fare and steamboat fare caused many people to decide in favor of steamboats.

Before steamers came into general use, a trip between New York City and Boston by stagecoach cost between five and eight cents a mile plus expenses along the way, the total cost averaging between twenty-five and thirty dollars. But by taking a steamboat from New York to Providence,

The stagecoach of the early 1800s. When passenger steamboats were put on the route between Providence and New York, coach lines became an important link between Providence, where the steamers landed, and Boston, the destination of many of the vessel's passengers. As the editor of the Providence Gazette *wrote: "We were rattled from Providence to Boston in four hours and fifty minutes—if any one wants to go faster he may send to Kentucky and charter a streak of lightning."*

Rhode Island, and then going on to Boston by coach, the fare was cut in half. A great reduction in traveling time was also a good reason to use a steamboat. From New York City to Boston by stage alone, took anywhere from four days to two weeks, and often longer depending on the weather and other conditions. With the use of the steamboat the time was cut to about twenty hours, or less than a day.

Also, the United States was a rapidly growing nation, and in the first and second decades of the nineteenth century people traveled much more than when John Fitch and James Rumsey were working on their steamboats shortly after the War of Independence. From earliest colonial times, settlements of European immigrants in America had been located on the seacoasts and river shores.

A stagecoach inn's sign. Such inns, where the traveler ate, drank and slept, were generally uncomfortable, crowded places. The "Entertainment" was mostly supplied free by the local fiddler.

By the beginning of the 1800s travel was heavy between these settlements, many of them having become large cities. In addition, there was a great westward movement stimulated by the Louisiana Purchase in 1803 and by the rapid growth in population. As steamboats continued to develop and improve, many people, even the poorest, preferred to use them rather than stage or wagon.

Until the number of steamboats increased sharply in the 1820s and '30s, most people used other means of water transportation. A variety of vessels were available for river travel. They ranged from canoes to enormous barges as large as Atlantic schooners. There were the popular flatboats, some measuring fifteen feet in width and from forty to a hundred feet in length, although most were smaller and many were simply crude rafts. An emigrant loaded his family and belongings on a flatboat and was carried down the river by the currents. When he reached his destination the flatboat was broken up and the lumber sold, or used as fuel or to build a house, or simply set adrift on the river.

A French botanist, F. A. Michaux, described

The popular western flatboat ranged from small, crude rafts to huge well-built vessels. Once they had served their purpose of carrying passengers and cargo down the river, they were usually broken up, the lumber being sold or used to build a house.

these flatboats in his *Travels to the West of the Allegheny Mountains,* published in 1805. "They are square in form," he wrote, "some longer than others; their sides are raised four feet and a half above the water . . . the two extremities are square, upon one of which is a kind of awning, under which the passengers shelter themselves when it rains."

There were keelboats: long, slender, shallow-draft boats that could carry up to thirty tons of cargo. Keelboats and barges took about six weeks to float down the Mississippi, and when poled and pulled back up the river by a crew, these vessels took about four months for the return trip. John James Audubon, the naturalist who produced such beautiful pictures of American birds and animals, gives a clear picture of how these boats were propelled up the river. He wrote: "The boat is again seen slowly advancing against the stream. It has reached the lower end of a sandbar, along the edge of which it is propelled by means of long poles, if the bottom be hard. Two men, called bowsmen, remain at the prow to assist, in concert with the steersman, in managing the boat and keeping its head right against the current. The rest place themselves on the land side of the footway of the vessel, put one end of their poles on the ground and the other against their shoulders and push with all their might. As each of the men reaches the stern, he crosses to the other side, runs along it and comes again to the landward side of the bow, where he recommences operations. The barge in the meantime is ascending at a rate not exceeding one mile in the hour."

People traveled the rivers of America on almost anything that could float: dugouts made from prodigiously large trees, skiffs, and sailing vessels of numerous shapes and sizes. Travel under sail was quieter and cleaner than travel by steamboat, and sailing ships continued to dominate coastal travel for years after river traffic was almost wholly conducted by steamboat.

But steamboats were a-coming, and the three men who, after Fitch, were most responsible for the development and acceptance of the steamboat in the United States formed a partnership in the winter of 1797. Their object was to build a steam-powered boat that would travel at five miles an hour. All three, the Chancellor of New York State (Robert R. Livingston), a colonel who fought in the War of Independence (John Stevens), and a young lawyer and engineer (Nicholas J. Roosevelt), came from families that had settled early in the American colonies.

Livingston, born in 1746, was a distinguished gentleman-farmer, politician, and diplomat. He

A barge being poled up the Mississippi River traveled at a rate not exceeding one mile an hour.

helped draft the Declaration of Independence and frame the constitution of the State of New York; he was the presiding judge of New York's Court of Chancery (thus the title of Chancellor); and he was the man who administered the oath of office when George Washington became the first President of the United States.

The Stevens family was also prominent in politics, the ratification of the Constitution, and the development of constitutional government in New Jersey. John Stevens, after whom the Stevens Institute of Technology in Hoboken is named, had a large estate in Hoboken. He was a lawyer, active politically as well as in many fields associated with transportation; he was also a horticulturist and a genius of mechanical engineering.

Livingston and Stevens had gone to college together and graduated together, and Stevens's sister Mary married Livingston in 1771. The brothers-in-law, despite their many differences of opinion, had a pleasant and affectionate regard for each other throughout their lives. Their correspondence reads like a record of the political and technological history of the period. It is rich in material concerning the development of all means of transportation of the time: steamboats, ferries, canals, stagecoaches, turnpikes, and railroads.

Stevens and Livingston were naturally drawn to Roosevelt, a man of advanced thinking in engineering. As early as 1793 Roosevelt was interested in developing foundries that could produce steam engines for American industries. He built a factory in Belleville, New Jersey, that he named Soho after the Boulton and Watt factory in England. He was the first man to put a steamboat into operation on the Mississippi, and with his young wife, Lydia Latrobe Roosevelt, the first to prove the great river navigable by steamboat.

Their project of 1797 was undertaken when Livingston received the steamboat monopoly in New York originally granted Fitch, and this, their first adventure into steamboat-building, was influenced by Fitch's efforts of which they were all conscious. Livingston designed a light, long, narrow craft; Stevens and Roosevelt did the major work on the engine. It took so long, however, that Livingston sent to Boulton and Watt in Birmingham, England, proposing to buy a Watt engine.

The sale was refused, for although a few had been exported the English government did not want other countries competing in industrial development: it was English policy to prevent all such technologically advanced devices from leaving the country.

The group experimented with a wheel at the side, at the stern, and, surprisingly, underwater below the keel. These tests did not go well; still hope of success was high in June of 1798 when Livingston wrote from Clermont, his New York estate, to Stevens: "I still anxiously expect the fruit of our labours in seeing you arrive here at the rate of five miles an hour . . ."

The trial of their vessel, named the *Polacca* (the

An engraving by Henry Robb of a batteau, usually used as a skiff by families for transporting cargo, or hired out for travel to places where barges or other river craft were not available.

polacca is a fast sailing vessel used in the Mediterranean), took place on the Passaic River in New Jersey and was witnessed by many people. It was "estimated" that the boat traveled at three to five miles an hour, but this estimate is probably inaccurate, for the partners decided to continue work on the boat because the engine was "too weak."

Correspondence among the three men continued, and there were other experiments. At one point Roosevelt suggested using paddle wheels at both sides of the boat, and eventually (on December 1, 1814), he was granted a patent for side paddle wheels. Stevens tried to improve the engine, believing the most serious shortcoming was that it had been built on the Watt plan and the pressure produced was not great enough to drive the machinery as well as it should. Many changes took place and a second trial was run. During this trial the light hull became so racked and weakened that the boat was unfit for further use. Stevens, Livingston, and Roosevelt, however, all continued individually to try to develop a practical steamboat, for as Livingston wrote, they had caught "steamboat fever."

In 1804 Stevens built a steamboat that mystified observers watching it move on the Hudson River. James Renwhich, a student at King's College (now Columbia University), was one of these observers. He wrote a friend: ". . .we saw. . .

Stevens's Little Juliana, *the steamboat that mystified observers in 1804.*

a vessel about the size of a Whitehall rowboat, in which there was a small engine but no visible means of propulsion." Many astonished people wondered, "How does it work?"

The answer was that Stevens's steamboat was driven by propellers, a feature that did not become common on steamers until the 1870s. A ship's propeller works by cutting forward in the water (similar to the way a turning screw pulls itself into wood) thus driving the vessel ahead. Another aspect of this boat called the *Little Juliana* that intrigued many people was the swift pace at which it moved in the water. The speed was due, in part, to a remarkable feature of the machinery Stevens had developed: the "safety" boiler.

Instead of using one large tank to supply steam for his engine, Stevens's boiler contained a hundred tubes; this innovation enormously increased the strength of the boiler that generated the steam. A year later Stevens's eldest son, John, improved on the water-tube boiler, and in 1856 it

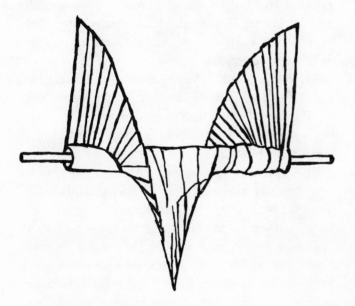

Early screw propellers were fashioned in many forms; the one above was carved in wood by Frédéric Sauvage in France.

was further perfected by Stephen Wilcox, making it much safer and more efficient for use on steam vessels.

The lack of tools and competent workmen in America during the early 1800s hindered Stevens himself from improving on this innovation. The occupation that was later to be known as "boiler-making" did not exist at that time. This disadvantage was greater in Stevens's case than with most engineers of that period, for he was attempting to produce a high-pressure engine. James Watt and other experimenters believed that pressure of two and a half to three pounds to the square inch was the maximum pressure to be used in working an engine. Watt flatly refused to build boilers that generated pressure greater than had been used in his early engines, for although he had used higher pressures he concluded that it would be too dangerous to go above the limit he had established earlier.

In an effort to get Boulton and Watt to build a high-pressure engine for his father, Stevens's son went to Birmingham. Watt's son told him that they never deviated from the principle, nor varied the construction from the first engines his father built. Stevens was working toward building an engine using pressure of from fifty to a hundred pounds to the inch, a figure that seemed not only incredibly dangerous, but impossible to achieve.

There was a man in America, Oliver Evans, whose achievements will be discussed later, who could have built a high-pressure engine for Stevens at the time the *Little Juliana* was operating on the waters of the Hudson, but Stevens, as did most steamboat enthusiasts of the time, wanted an engine of his own design.

Stevens, in fact, was attempting to produce steamboats of such advanced technological design that the mechanical means to accomplish this end were not available to anyone in America until later in the century. It is interesting to note that when the first "modern" steamships were built years later, they incorporated all the features Stevens considered necessary on a "proper" steamboat. Although he only partially succeeded with the *Little Juliana,* Stevens went on experimenting and in a few years was producing the fastest steamboats in the world.

Robert Livingston also continued to search out a method of building a practical steamboat: as newspapers of the time said, the steamboat project was "the Chancellor's hobby." In 1800 he was appointed Ambassador to France, and while in Paris was introduced to Robert Fulton as "just the man you want." Robert Fulton was born in Pennsylvania in 1765 and trained in Philadelphia and London as an artist. He took to engineering and

worked on canal construction in England, but soon drifted into the field of armament development. Fulton often said that he did so because he believed that if he perfected the submarine, mines, and torpedoes he could bring a halt to all war at sea by making naval activity so risky that war would have to be abolished.

The French government granted him money to work on the submarine that had earlier been developed by the American pioneer of underwater attack David Bushnell. Like many inventors, Fulton was hardly ever ready to acknowledge a debt to a previous experimenter. For instance, when dealing with someone who knew nothing about Bushnell's work, Fulton would claim to be the creator of the submarine—but when he wrote to an informed American he made a point of mentioning Bushnell.

This trait appears again when Fulton claimed that he was the inventor of the steamboat, although previously, when dealing with people who knew better, he merely said that he had made improvements in steamboats. These false claims of originality should not diminish Fulton's stature, for he and Livingston were responsible for the first financially successful steamboat, thus encouraging many people to enter the field. Besides, such claims of inventions being original were com-

One of Robert Fulton's first sketches of a steamboat. Although at first glance it looks like a rowboat, its design, including the presence of portholes, proves it to be a large sailing vessel. According to the scale of the ship the paddle wheel would have been over 30 feet in diameter.

monly made in many fields for a very practical reason: to protect the improvements in these inventions that *were* original, and in turn, ensure an inventor's source of income and help repay him for the time, labor, and money he extended while working on these improvements. Edison's claim to the invention of the incandescent electric light falls in the same class and was made to protect the great inventor's unique solution to the problem of artificial light.

Fulton was clever at developing refinements in devices already in existence, and this is what he did with the submarine. In 1801 he built the *Nautilus;* with it he succeeded in blowing up an old schooner by placing an explosive charge below the waterline. The slowness of the work, and the opposition of French naval officers (who thought this method of attack deceitful), put an end to Fulton's submarine experiments, although he continued to work on the development of mines and torpedoes. It was at this time that he met Livingston.

On October 10, 1802, they signed a partnership agreement that provided for construction of a steamboat to carry sixty passengers and run at eight miles an hour. The boat was built and put on trial August 9, 1803, on the river Seine. It moved at a speed of only three or four miles an hour. In describing the plans to the *Conservatoire des Arts et Métiers,* Fulton wrote: "You will find nothing new" about this boat. Unlike Fitch, Fulton working in France where so many early steamboat schemes had originated had a number of models available including one made by Jouffroy and Fitch's own drawings which he had left behind in France.

The experiments on the Seine did not meet the goals that had been set, but the partnership was kept intact. Fulton left France and went to England where he offered the government his designs for underwater warfare devices. Although

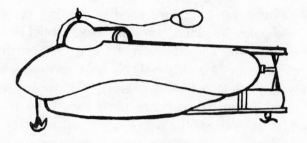

Fulton's Nautilus: *the explosive charge was carried in the float being towed along outside the submarine.*

the English had no intention of using these devices, they paid Fulton a good deal of money for them in order to prevent other governments from developing them. Besides paying for the plans, the English allowed Fulton to buy and export a Watt engine.

The possession of this engine in America was a great advantage for Livingston and Fulton, as engines produced commercially in their own country were not as reliable or as well constructed. The Watt engine was put in a hull built in the shipyard of Charles Browne in New York. Paddle wheels and machinery were put into place, and the steamboat made its way up the Hudson River in August of 1807.

A spectator, H. Freeland, has left an account of what some people thought of when the Livingston-Fulton steamer was seen for the first time. "Some imagined it to be a sea-monster while others did not hesitate to express their belief that it was a sign of the approaching judgment." This was not much different from what Indians thought of the first steamboats they saw. As we shall see, however, the first steamer on the Hudson was usually greeted with cheers.

Another interesting sidelight on the way people reacted to the first steamboats is shown by a notice that appeared in an early 1800 newspaper report which stated: "Sundry persons concerned in the shad and herring fishery in the Potomac have presented a petition to the Virginia legislature, praying that steam-boats may be forbidden to run in the month of April [when shad and herring come in from the ocean to spawn in coastal rivers]; because, they say, that the noise of the boat, which may be heard several miles, and the agitation of the air and water drive the fish away." What a terrible racket these boats must have made to "be heard several miles." To be on one must have been a deafening experience.

The official New York State certificate assuring the monopoly to Livingston and Fulton was issued at Albany on September 5, 1807. This certificate covered the second trip the steamboat made up the Hudson. This voyage began on Friday, September 4, 1807. The certificate very precisely states: "At eighteen minutes before seven o'clock, the North River boat left New York, landed one passenger at Tarrytown, (twenty-five miles,) arrived at Newburgh (sixty-three miles) at four o'clock in the afternoon, landed one passenger there, arrived at Clermont, (one hundred miles,) where two passengers, one of whom was Mr. Fulton, were landed, at fifteen minutes before two o'clock in the morning, and arrived at Albany at twenty-seven minutes past eleven o'clock, making the time twenty-eight hours and three-quarters, distance one hundred and fifty miles."

This official certificate was signed by twelve men, among them Judge John Q. Wilson, who later left an account of what the trip was like. The forward part of the boat was covered by a deck that afforded shelter to the hands. The after part was fitted up, in a rough manner, for passengers. The entrance to the cabin was from the stern, in front of the steersman, who worked a tiller as in an ordinary sloop. There were only twelve berths. Judge Wilson describes Fulton by saying: "His remarkably clear and sharp voice was heard above the hum of the multitude and the noise of the engine; his step was confident and decided . . ."

Judge Wilson was very much impressed with Fulton, especially by his calmness and the unusual brilliance of his flashing eyes.

Unlike many other reports that have come down to us concerning the reception of the steamboat, Judge Wilson's is not only more complete, but stresses the cheering crowds along the river. When the steamboat began the voyage, he states: "as she turned up the river and was fairly under weigh, there arose such a huzza [shout] as ten thousand throats never gave before. The passengers returned the cheer" but Fulton stood silent. He goes on to say: "As we passed West Point, the whole garrison was out, and cheered as we passed. At Newburgh it seemed as if all Orange county was collected there; the whole side-hill city seemed animated with life." This is a much more reasonable account of events than the colorful but prejudiced tales of fainting Dutchmen, fleeing Baptists, moaning blacks, and witlessly frightened farmers who thought the devil was coming upriver in a flaming mill.

On May 14, 1808, the next year, Robert Livingston applied for relicensing at the New York Custom House. The application or "enrollment" stated that the vessel was the *North River Steamboat of Clermont,* giving the area of operation, the class of vessel, and the place of residence of the holder of the monopoly. In newspaper reports, as Fitch's boat had been, it was referred to as the "Steamboat," or the "North River Steamboat": it was only after a number of years that the name *Clermont* began to appear, and into the 1870s the name was almost always enclosed by quotes, the *"Clermont."*

The relicensing application stated that the new

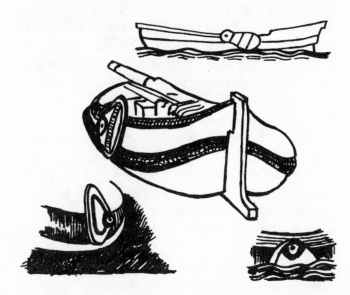

Leeboards on the side of a vessel. When lowered into the water (lower right) *leeboards prevent a ship from being forced off course when a strong wind is blowing toward the side of the vessel.*

"enrollment" was being taken out because the boat was enlarged to 149 feet in length, 17 feet 11 inches in breadth, and that it had one deck and two masts. An interesting feature of the first boat, which did not appear on the remodeled one, was a set of leeboards—two large oval-shaped boards placed toward the center at each side. Leeboards were lowered into the water to prevent a ship from being forced off course when a strong wind came from the side. The wheels on the original Livingston-Fulton steamer were uncovered.

Some idea of what the remodeled boat looked like can be gotten by reading a report of it in an issue of the Hudson, New York, newspaper the *Hudson Bee* that appeared early in July of 1808. *"The Steam Boat,"* the article reads, "is certainly an interesting curiosity to strangers. To see this large and apparently unwieldy machine, without oars or sail, propelled thro' the element by invisible agency, at a rate of four miles in an hour, would be a novelty in any quarter of the globe . . ." It goes on to describe the twenty-horse-power engine, the copper boiler "8 or 10 feet in length" and the wheels on each side, "similar to those of water mills, and under cover they are moved backward or forward, separately or together, at pleasure." This is a feature concerning steamboats that has often been said to have been

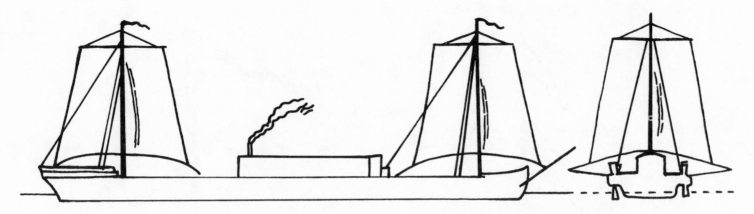

A copy of Fulton's own drawing of the Clermont *of 1807, the original of which is in the collection of the New York Historical Society, New York City.*

discovered by accident years later, but like many stories dealing with early steamboats, it is more romantic than accurate.

The *Hudson Bee* article goes on to disclose that: "Her accommodations (52 births [berths], besides sofas, &c.) are said to be equal or superior to any vessel that floats on the river." The forty extra berths built into the vessel, along with the sofas, were well used, for the article states that the average passage takes thirty-two hours and the number of passengers between eighty and a hundred. The *Washington National Intelligencer* of August 1808 enlarges on the story by stating: "We are rejoyced to hear that this useful invention [steamboats], the favorite of the people of New York, is meeting with the most encouraging success." It goes on to say that on the 2nd of August there were 115 passengers; on the 9th, 104 passengers; on the 16th of August there were 141, and "fifty passengers applied who could not be received on board."

The steamboat was a success, and soon Livingston and Fulton had the *Car of Neptune* in operation and then the *Raritan* (which was unfortunately sunk in a gale in January 1810). The *Clermont* itself stayed in service until July 1814, when steamboats had become a common sight on

John Stevens's Phoenix.

the Hudson. By then Livingston had been dead for over a year, and Fulton was to die the next January.

Meanwhile John Stevens was also making progress in developing improvements in steamboat transportation, along with his advanced schemes and experiments in railroad construction, bridge building, and sanitation. With such men as Franklin, and other original and brilliant thinkers, Stevens helped the young United States grow into a strong, well-developed nation. After the *Little Juliana* of 1804 he built a paddle boat "on a very small scale" and another boat, a steam ferry about forty feet long. His first large boat was named the *Phoenix*, sometimes called the *Phenix*. The monopoly granted by New York to Livingston prevented Stevens from operating on the Hudson or Long Island Sound, so Stevens had to use another area to put his steamboat on a working schedule: he chose the Delaware River.

In order to get the *Phoenix* to its destination in Philadelphia, Stevens was forced to travel out into the Atlantic Ocean, down the coast of New Jersey, then around Cape May. Today there is nothing astonishing about such a brief voyage; it could be accomplished by a steam ferry boat or a small tug without difficulty because of their powerful engines; but in the early 1800s a trip of this sort made by a steamboat was believed impossible, and if not impossible extremely dangerous. One observer said that he would "as soon volunteer for an expedition to the moon as go on that cruise in a little 'steam kettle.'" (Steam kettles and stinkpots were two of the various early names used to disparage steamboats.) Some said the steamboat would be smashed to pieces by the ocean's waves, while others thought that once the *Phoenix* got out into the ocean away from the safe, sheltered bays of New York, it would come to a stand-still as its machinery would not be strong enough to work against the wind and waves it would encounter.

Stevens hired an experienced man to take the *Phoenix* to sea, Captain Moses Rogers. Stevens's son Robert, just twenty-one, accompanied Rogers on this adventure to make sure the engine was properly looked after. To assist the steamboat Stevens sent along a tender, a vessel with sail carrying emergency supplies. The record of the voyage that began on June 10, 1809, has a significant entry repeated many times: "The tender still absent," or, "No appearance yet of our tender." The steamboat went ahead during calms and even when the wind was squally.

The *Phoenix* made its way down the coast slowly, putting into port when the weather was too rough. The trip to Philadelphia took fourteen days, during which time the weather was almost continually bad. But rain, heavy seas, and a gale did not prevent Stevens's boat from arriving in Philadelphia where it was fitted out with stores and made its first trip to Trenton on July 9. Henry Voight, who had worked so long and hard with Fitch on earlier steamboats, and who was now in charge of the U.S. Mint in Philadelphia, wrote: "The Steamboat has made a trip to Trenton yesterday, & performed it 8 hours up and 8 hours coming back."

The speed was only three and a half miles an

An early eastern steamer.

hour, but with improvements made by Stevens and his sons the *Phoenix* was soon going five miles an hour. It was not long before steamboats were going much faster and routes on Chesapeake Bay and elsewhere were coming into existence. Passengers more and more often went by steamboat rather than by stage, for as Stevens wrote, the difference between these means of travel was that: "In one case the passenger arrives fatigued and unfitted for business, in the other—unfatigued."

Stevens also said that steamboats had "set people all agog." He was right, for people soon realized how inexpensive and comfortable steamboat travel was, and soon, too, people wanted to operate steamboat lines wherever they chose without having to get the consent of the owners of the Hudson monopoly. They took the monopolists to court and many cases were fought and lost until February 1824, when Chief Justice John Marshall declared that all barriers to free navigation on the rivers of the United States to boats propelled by "fire or steam" were removed. No state could restrict its river use to special interests or particular groups. When this decision was given the Livingston and Fulton company could no longer control the building and use of steamboats in the East as they had for years: steamboats had come of age.

CHAPTER 5

Pioneers on the Western Rivers

THE DEVELOPMENT of the steamboat was not sudden and spectacular, although there were dramatic adventures and achievements by outstanding individuals whose actions made progress possible in the field. The story of Nicholas J. Roosevelt's journey down the Mississippi on the first steamboat to make the arduous trip is an example of such an achievement. John Fitch had the conquest of the Mississippi in mind when experimenting with steamboats on the Delaware. And, the *American and Commercial Daily Advertiser* reported on August 17, 1807, that: "Mr. Fulton's ingenious Steam Boat, invented with a view of the navigation of the Mississippi . . ." was ready to sail. Western rivers were swifter and more of a challenge than the rivers on which the early experimenters worked. Also, if the Ohio, Missouri, and Mississippi could be made as navigable as tidewater, as Fitch wrote in 1786, then the steamboat would "make our vast territory on these waters an inconceivable Fund in the treasure of the United States."

It is somewhat fashionable, especially in some fields of entertainment, to depict Easterners in the settlement of the West as soft and unable to cope with rugged western conditions. New Englanders, New Yorkers, and others are often ridiculed as being either too gentle or too stupid to deal with the harsh frontier environment. This is to ignore the facts and distort history, for it was the brave, determined, and intelligent Easterners such as Nicholas Roosevelt who made the movement into the interior successful in the first place. (Daniel Boone, for instance, was born in eastern Pennsylvania, and only settled in Kentucky when he was about forty years old.)

The story of Roosevelt's voyage appears in pamphlets and newspaper clippings yellow and brittle with age. In 1809 Livingston and Fulton asked Roosevelt to undertake a reconnaissance trip on the Ohio and Mississippi to study currents, river conditions, and trade statistics, to see if a steamboat could be used profitably on these waters. Roosevelt had just married, and he and his wife decided to make the voyage of exploration their honeymoon trip. In May 1809 he built a flatboat at Pittsburgh, which Mrs. Roosevelt described in a letter as being "a huge box."

As they slowly traveled down the river Roose-

Interior of a flatboat in the early 1800s.

velt questioned everyone he could about the possibility of a steamboat working on these swift rivers. Businessmen, lawyers, politicians, boatmen, and pilots all thought the project was not feasible. The voyage down the river took six months, and in spite of the lack of encouragement he had received, Roosevelt was confident a steam vessel could conquer the Mississippi. When he and his wife returned to New York by sailing ship from New Orleans, he gave a favorable report to Livingston and Fulton. In 1810 he returned to Pittsburgh with the plans for a steamboat designed by Fulton.

With him he brought experienced steamboat men who had worked for Fulton for the past few years. Once the hull was finished the engine and paddle wheels had to be installed, then the cabins were fitted out, a ladies' cabin aft, and one for gentlemen forward. The boat was named *New Orleans*, but it was often simply called the *Orleans*. It had cost nearly $40,000 dollars. This was a great sum of money then, but soon steam vessels were being built that cost much more. In the early years of steamboating owners were fond of quoting and advertising the amount of money their vessels cost. A value of $75,000 was a "grand" steamboat, $55,000 was a "good" steamer, and as the value decreased the elegance also decreased.

By the 1820s there were steamboats being constructed for $175,000.

The trials for the *New Orleans* did not take place until September 1811. Then the Roosevelts, living in the after cabin, began their voyage. Along with them were a captain, an engineer, a pilot, and ten crew members aboard. They set out from Pittsburgh on October 1, 1811, and reached Louisville four days later after a stop at Cincinnati. All early steamboat builders seem to have had a touch of showmanship. (Later, when Vanderbilt, Drew, and Fisk were on the scene the shows were spectaculars.) Roosevelt was no exception. The people at Cincinnati had said goodbye by telling the Roosevelts that they were sorry they would not be seeing them again, because they might go down the river in a steamboat, but it was foolish to believe they would ever be able to come back up. Once down as far as Louisville, Roosevelt ordered a return to Cincinnati to prove the *New Orleans* could navigate upriver. This story is merely legend: Roosevelt, waiting for the falls to rise so that the steamer could pass over them without too much difficulty, ran an excursion between the two cities. The fare was a dollar and the excursion proved a profitable, amusing interlude.

Mrs. Roosevelt gave birth the last week of November just as the depth of the water at the

The *New Orleans, adapted here from an old sketch, was probably a side-wheeler. Early artists often used their imagination to depict an event.*

falls (actually a series of rapids) would allow the deep draft of the boat to pass over: at the shallowest part the boat's safety margin was only a few inches. Friends suggested that she and her child travel overland and meet the boat farther down, but she remained aboard. People lined the shore as the steamboat proceeded on its dangerous passage over the falls; they were waiting for the ship to be ripped open, but with an experienced pilot aboard the hazardous trip was made without incident.

After anchoring below the falls, those aboard felt the first shock of an earthquake, possibly the greatest ever to occur in a non-volcanic region. It was centered near New Madrid, Missouri, and was felt over two-thirds of the area of the United States. During the following days they made their way through the dreadful desolation caused by the quake, where forests had sunk and huge lakes formed in their stead, and the course of rivers was severely altered. During this time the boat was repeatedly shaken by shocks and at times great waves drenched the decks.

Each day, early in the afternoon, the steamer was tied up at the bank while the crew went ashore to cut wood for the fires and boiler. One afternoon they tied up at an island, gathered wood, ate, and went to bed. Suddenly awakened during the night, they discovered to their amazement that the island had disappeared. The boat was being pulled underwater by the tree to which the cable was secured. They hastily cut the cable, and getting up pressure continued down the treacherously altered river. Gradually the earthquake subsided and they safely reached Natchez.

When the *New Orleans* left Natchez it was carrying a shipment of cotton, the first goods to go by steamboat on a western river. In January of 1812 it began making profitable weekly trips between New Orleans and Natchez; the fare upriver was twenty-five dollars, downriver, eighteen. After two years of service between the two cities (approximately three hundred miles apart on the river), the *New Orleans* was impaled on a stump at Baton Rouge due to rapidly receding waters. Furious efforts to free the steamboat ripped the hole wider, and the *New Orleans* filled with water and sank.

When considered against the background of the time, Roosevelt's achievement gives some idea of the significance of steamboats on the Mississippi. Not only did the use of the steamboat make possible the quick distribution of goods and people in wilderness areas, it helped eliminate the earlier feeling of isolation and encouraged a national feeling—an American identity on a grand scale. The people of the new West led lives which were shaped by their unsettled environment. It was a different life-style, but with the use of steamboats they could keep in touch with the East where the money and manufactured goods were, and where national political decisions were made. The western settler's national interests were therefore allied more closely to the interests of the

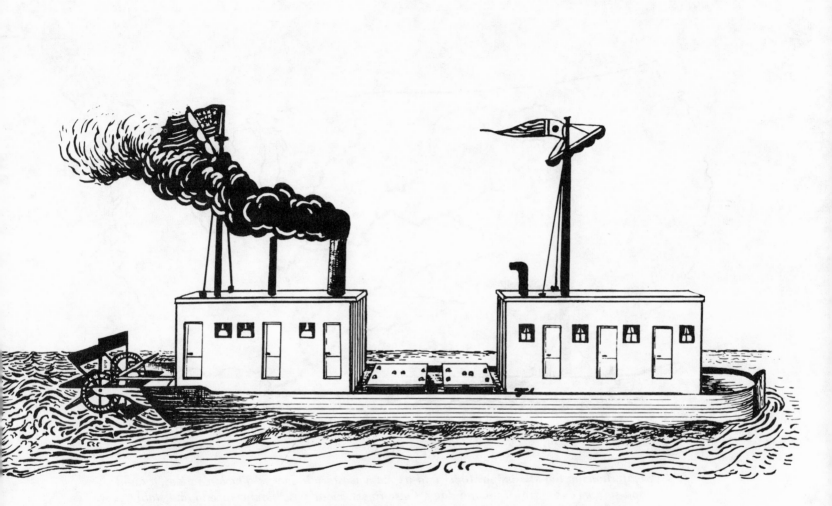

The New Orleans, *based on a model in the Carnegie Institute collection in Pittsburgh.*

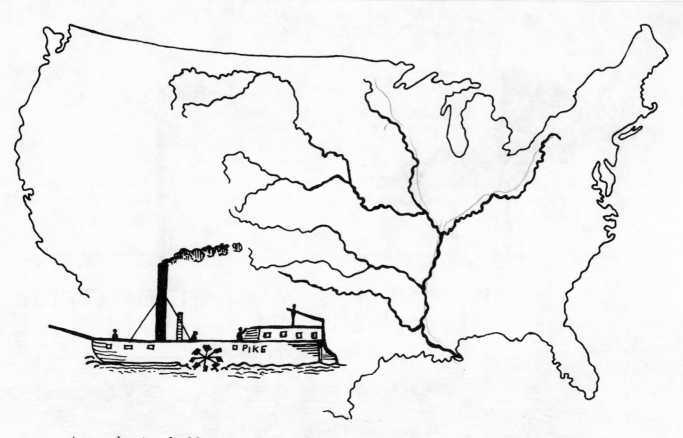

A map showing the Mississippi River and its main western branches. The steamboat, a rapid
and safe means of travel up and down these rivers, made possible the speedy and stable
development of the American West. The Zebulon M. Pike, pictured with
the map, was the first steamer to reach St. Louis (1817).

earlier settled areas than they might have been if the time/distance ratio had been greater.

The steamboat was able to help tie together the American nation because the Mississippi River, and the branch rivers flowing into it, covered not only the near West, but the far West. The Missouri, Ohio, Arkansas, Red, and other rivers presented a natural highway for immigrants and goods. These branch rivers reached to the foot of the Rocky Mountains and within a few hundred miles of the Pacific Ocean. The course of the branches in the West was southeast, moving toward New Orleans. What was required to open these rivers to settlement and stable development quickly, was a rapid and safe means of travel up and down them as they ran through the wilderness: the steamboat was the answer.

The Spanish and the Indians were still in control of most of the United States in the 1810–20 decade, and the West was sparsely settled in a broad sweep that began with Lake Erie, followed the Ohio until it joined the Mississippi, went up the Mississippi, then followed the Missouri. With the introduction of the steamboat, pioneers went farther up these branch rivers, and their settlements depended on river transportation for rapid development through trade.

The areas between the settled rivers were lightly populated. The opening of the plains areas did not take place until the river settlements had been made secure. In those early years of the 1800s the people from the East were colonizing Ohio and the Northwest Territory (roughly Indiana and Illinois); people from Maryland, Virginia, Pennsylvania, and other seaboard areas were moving into Kentucky and Tennessee. The adventurous were settling in the Michigan Territory. The great surge of European immigrants into these western sections of the country did not begin in earnest until much later.

The steamboat carried many of these eastern emigrants to their destinations, then carried their saleable products, such as flour, honey, bears' oil, and furs to St. Louis or Pittsburgh. Furs went to New York and from there to London and Paris; cotton went down the Mississippi to New Orleans and then to the mills of England and France. Cloth, guns, nails, furniture, and other manufactured goods (pianos and prefabricated houses were popular items) arrived from eastern sections quickly and cheaply.

In the years before the development of the railroads if such items went overland their cost increased enormously. Freight by land was handled by teamsters who traveled only during the day. It was a slow and expensive means of transport suited for fairly valuable, non-spoilable articles. Also, the only fairly good road of any importance going west was the Cumberland and National Road which was completed in 1818 and ran from either Baltimore or Washington, D.C., to Wheeling, Virginia (later West Virginia).

At various times Westerners in Congress tried to put bills for road construction through Congress, but the bills were not enacted into law because such laws were at first believed unconstitutional. Road building was considered a function of local governments. States did begin building their own roads and canals westward during the 1820s, but the total lack of such roads and canals in the rapidly developing West created a need for a reliable means of transportation: with the introduction of the steamboat the rivers of America became the national highways.

Just how important the steamboat was to the pioneer Westerner is clearly expressed by William Peterson, who wrote in *Steamboating on the Upper Mississippi:* "If a captain arrived twice during a season he was welcomed as a friend; if he made several trips he was looked upon as a brother; and if he appeared in the trade two successive seasons he was almost deified."

The *New Orleans* was the first steamboat to travel the Mississippi on a regular run. But from 1811 to 1817 few steamboats were launched in the West. This was not only because the monopoly granted by the Territory of Orleans had been given to the Livingston-Fulton interests, but also because the swiftness of these rivers called for a highly powered boat.

John Stevens and others had experimented with high-pressure engines, but the successful high-pressure engine which came into use and made steamboating on western rivers possible was developed from the engines built by Oliver Evans. Born in Delaware in 1755, he left school at fourteen to apprentice himself to a wagon-maker. A few years later he learned of the existence of steam engines, and although he was poor and lacked education he determined to build such engines and convert the wagons he was building into steam carriages. His position was similar to that of a young man today who at seventeen might decide to manufacture his own space craft.

Evans experimented in other directions as well; when he was barely twenty-one he perfected a machine for turning out toothed cards used in carding wool. At twenty-five he went to work for his brothers in their flour mill in Wilmington. The machines he invented for the mill enabled the grain and meal to move from machine to machine without manual assistance.

His mind was fertile and his inventions practical, but he had no money and could not find financial backing for any of his schemes. Also, many people strongly opposed his inventions as "unnatural" and tending to put men out of work. In 1787 Maryland allowed Evans the exclusive right to use his mill machinery, as well as his "steam carriage," on the grounds that these things "could injure no one."

After working on his steam carriage for thirteen years he put the invention aside to build stationary engines. By 1802, when he was forty-seven years old, he had produced a successful high-pressure engine. It was much lighter and more compact than any engine built at the time. It was called a half-beam engine, and because of the jumpy movement of this half-beam (the Newcomen and Watt full beam was cut in half at the middle and the missing half replaced by a moving arm) it was nicknamed the "grasshopper." Evans and others thought it so successful that the next year he started in business as an engine builder.

It is often reported that Evans then built and shipped an engine and machinery to New Orleans to be used for installation in the hull of a ship. How the story proclaiming Evans responsible for this boat originally started is not clear. Evans, a grand showman, never makes any mention of this

feat, and if he had been involved in such an adventure in 1803 he certainly would have mentioned it, for he very vocally mentioned his other steamboat adventures.

There was a permit issued in 1803 at New Orleans for the construction of a steamboat. James McKeever, who took out this permit, did construct a steamboat with the help of his partner Louis Valcour. There were three Newcomen-type steam engines then in operation in New Orleans. For a number of reasons neither a Watt nor an Evans engine would have been available. (The English government was still severely restricting the export of the Watt engine. Evans had just begun his engine building that year; his patent was not granted until 1804; and the engines he built were for his own use in mills and on his steam dredge.) An engine was built for the McKeever-Valcour boat and installed: the Mississippi dropped drastically just afterward and the boat was left high and dry. Their capital exhausted, the partners removed the engine and rented it to a William Donaldson, who operated a saw mill.

In 1804, however, Evans did put one of his engines to work on an amphibious steam-propelled vehicle which was used successfully as a dredge for the city of Philadelphia. This land-sea steam contraption was called the *Orukter Am-*

phibolos (amphibious digger). It was concerning this steam-dredge that Evans later wrote (when Fulton was claiming the invention of so many features of the steamboat): "I exhibited a steamboat, steamwaggon in the year 1804 in Delaware and on Market Street to thousands of spectators before Fulton ever done anything of the kind."

Evans had a great deal of difficulty in keeping others from using his engines without payment or credit to him. In August of 1817 he wrote to various newspaper editors, giving the following account of his discoveries: "Citizens attend! . . . This discovery [the high pressure engine] has recently been so openly attacked that the inventor is compelled to defend it. Therefore, I announce that more than forty years ago, I discovered the principles and afterwards the means of applying the great and advantageous principle in nature of the rapid *increase of the elastic power of steam,* by geometrical progression, by the small *increase of heat in the water,* by arithmetical progression, and thereby to lessen the consumption of fuel, the size and weight of the steam engine to suit for steam boats." This report, which appeared in the *American Daily Advertiser* late in August 1817, goes on to give Evans's detailed description of the engine and the boiler, and how they could be used to make steamboats safer. He sent the report to the various editors in the hope that his engine would save lives and money (by being adopted on steamboats, which it was, but with modifications). As Evans wrote, he had spent "a long and laborious life, of arduous and intense study to discover the principles, defray the expenses of testing them and to secure my right by patent, and to establish extensive works to manufacture the steam engines, both at Philadelphia and Pittsburgh, to supply the demand, that therefore by this publication I do not mean to relinquish or impair any of my vested and lawful rights, as a patentee, discoverer and inventor."

By 1807 Evans established the Mars Iron Works where for many years the high-pressure engines in use in the United States were built. Unfortunately for Evans his first engines were bought and copies of them made without his consent, and without any profit to him. Most of the high-pressure engines were simply pirated Evans models. The engines Evans himself built were phenomenal machines. The boilers on the one he constructed for the Fairmount Waterworks in Philadelphia yielded steam at an incredible two hundred-pounds pressure. He had proved that such engines could be manufactured and that they were safer than earlier experimenters believed—if they were not abused. Still, at the time, few steamboat builders in the eastern United States and in Europe were willing to change from the low-pressure Watt engines. Those who did, such as Stevens, met with resistance and discouragement, for eastern steamboats were used primarily as passenger vessels designed for comfort, not speed. In the West the high-pressure engine was used because of the currents, and also because the western boats were primarily used to carry heavy freight loads.

Still there were exceptions, and during the next fifty or sixty years low-pressure engines were often used on the Mississippi and its branch rivers, just as high-pressure engines were often used in the East, contrary to common belief. The second steamboat the Livingston-Fulton interests put on the Mississippi had a low-pressure engine as the earlier *New Orleans* had had. This second vessel was the *Vesuvius*. It was launched with high hopes of success as the notice in *Niles' Weekly Register* of May 21, 1814, shows. It reads: "This morning [April 22, 1814] the steamboat *Vesuvius* intended as a regular trader between New Orleans and the falls of Ohio, left Pittsburgh. A considerable fresh [rise] in the river renders it probable, that notwithstanding the great size and draft of the vessel, she will pass the falls without difficulty, after which she will meet with no obstruction in the rest of her passage. There is now on the stocks here, just ready to be launched, a boat [the *Buffalo*, launched in July] adapted to the navigation of the Ohio above the falls, which will be finished in time to meet the *Vesuvius* on her return from New Orleans at the falls. The boats were built by Mr. Fulton under the agency of Messrs. [Edward] Livingston [Robert's brother; a lawyer, once Mayor of New York City, later a Representative and Senator, and from 1833 to 1835 Minister to France as his brother had been] and [Benjamin Henry] Latrobe [an engineer and architect, father of Nicholas Roosevelt's wife, Lydia] for companies, who have vested very large capitals in the establishment. The departure of the *Vesuvius* is a very important event, not only for this place but for the whole western part of the union, and its influence will be felt over the whole United States."

For some reason the *Vesuvius* did not actually leave Pittsburgh until the next morning, Saturday, April 23. Then it went down to New Orleans on an uneventful voyage. But on its return upriver it was grounded and not floated off until the winter floods several months later. Returning to New Orleans, it went aground again and was stuck tight for another ten weeks. The next year it caught fire and burned. Such events were common enough in the early days of steamboating.

Henry Miller Shreve, the man who was in good part responsible for the acceptance and development of the Mississippi River steamboat, was born in New Jersey in 1785. He was taken when young to western Pennsylvania, and as a youth worked on barges and flatboats on western rivers. The type of steamboat he worked toward developing

French's steamer Enterprise, *which, under the command of Captain Shreve, was the first steamboat to ascend the Mississippi from New Orleans to Louisville. The original print from which this drawing was made may be inaccurate; the vessel may well have been a side-wheeler.*

was a high-pressure freight carrier overflowing with goods and people in constant activity: it looked like a rectangular two-layered pound cake. These western steamboats were used by the poorest emigrants hopeful of building a new life in undeveloped country, and also were used by the most elegant and refined planters and businessmen of the time: this river craft was a world of its own.

Fayette County, Pennsylvania, where young Shreve grew up is bounded by the Monongahela and Youghiogheny Rivers which flow north and join, then meet the Allegheny at Pittsburgh where the river becomes the Ohio. Growing up in this area, it is no wonder that Shreve became a river man. At fourteen he began his early trading trips down the Monongahela and Ohio into the West. He took the profits earned in this trade and at twenty-eight invested in his first steamboat company. This was Daniel French's steamboat company that built the *Comet.* In the spring of 1814 the *Comet* steamed to New Orleans; it then made two trips to Natchez, but was not a success so it was sold and dismantled.

The same year Shreve became part owner in a second steamboat designed by French called the *Enterprise,* an eighty-foot sternwheeler built at Brownsville, Pennsylvania. Shreve became one of the captains operating this vessel, and on his first voyage carried supplies down the river to General Andrew Jackson's army at New Orleans. After valuable service to the American forces fighting the last battle of the War of 1812, Shreve undertook the first long upriver voyage to Louisville, Kentucky: he covered nearly 1,500 miles in twenty-five days. The report of this voyage in *Niles' Weekly Register* added a significant fact: "It is thought that the freight from New Orleans to Louisville will soon be reduced to $3.50 per c. [hundredweight]." This was a fifty percent reduction in the freight rate, a cut that would increase river shipments enormously. Shreve's voyage had been a swift one. The usual time later established for early Mississippi steamers covering the same distance was between thirty and thirty-five days or sometimes longer due to frequent stops for passengers, fueling, and freight along the way.

A restraining action was brought against the owners of the *Enterprise* by the Livingston-Fulton interests. The vessel was seized, released, then seized again. It was seized a number of times, until the owners realized it could not be operated on the Mississippi.

In the spring of 1816 another steamer named the *Enterprise* sailed from Savannah to Charleston, South Carolina. It arrived at Charleston on June 23, and: "Being the first [steam] boat ever seen at Charleston, she excites great curiosity and admiration. Ten years hence, such a boat will be no rarity anywhere in the United States—where there is water to float one." This was the second steamer to timidly venture into the Atlantic, and although no real gain to oceanic steam development, it is interesting to note that the easy passage between Savannah and Charleston only took thirty-one hours.

A report of the next boat in which Shreve had an interest appeared in an Ohio newspaper on June 6, 1816. "On Monday evening last, the steamboat *Washington* sailed from Wheeling for New Orleans, under the command of Captain Henry M. Shreve. She got under way about five o'clock, and in forty-five minutes made *nine miles*.

"The steamboat *Washington* was built at Wheeling by Mr. George White. Her keel was laid on the 10th of September last. In August all her timbers were growing in the woods. [This was a favorite expression of the period; it appears in many accounts of ship construction.] She is 148 feet in length. Her main cabin is 60 feet; she has three private rooms, besides a commodious bar room. She is furnished and equipped in a very superior style. . . She is owned by Messrs. Neal Gillespie and Robert Clark of Brownsville, Messrs. Noah Zane and George White of Wheeling, and

Captain Shreve. Many who have seen and examined her, announce her the finest steam vessel on the western waters. Her steam power is applied upon an entirely new principle, exceedingly simple and light (high-pressure). She has no balance wheel, and her whole engine possessing a power of one hundred horses, weighs only nine thousand pounds. It is the invention of Captain Shreve."

The construction of the *Washington* introduced the layer-cake fashion that became so popular:

The Washington, *launched in 1816, introduced a second deck on western steamers.*

there was a main deck above the hold, an upper deck, and the hurricane deck. No one knows who designed the *Washington*. Shreve himself seemed mainly interested in the construction of the engine —newspaper reports have him checking it a number of times and making special trips in order to do so. (This engine, of course, was not the invention of Shreve, but of Oliver Evans. Both French and Shreve used the Evans engines with their own modifications.)

The boilers for the engine were placed on the main deck, the engine was in the hold, and the hull of the vessel did not differ from the earlier steamboats built in the West along sailing ship lines. It was said to be "built like a ship," not like a flatboat. Gradually the whole of the machinery was put on the main deck; guards, or fenders, were added as extensions of the main deck on both sides beyond the hull itself. The guards became a part of the main deck, making it more spacious and also protecting the side paddle wheels.

Before the *Washington* left on its first voyage there was an explosion aboard caused by a faulty cylinder. It was the first of the many steamboat explosions in which lives were lost. Repairs were made and Shreve took the *Washington* on its first trip from Pittsburgh to New Orleans, rounding back to Louisville, all in forty-one days.

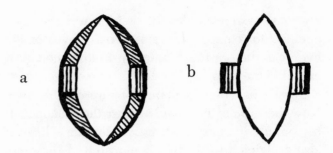

Looking down from above: (a) the guards on an American steamer, and (b) European steamer without guards: one of the many differences between early American and European steamboats.

An important event in steamboat development in the West occurred when Shreve arrived at New Orleans with the *Washington*: he had no sooner tied up when the Livingston-Fulton interests had him arrested for infringing on the monopoly given them by the Territory of Orleans. Edward Livingston offered Shreve an interest in the monopoly if he would join them and avoid a court case, but Shreve refused. Livingston then sued Shreve. When the case finally came before the U.S. District Court for Louisiana, the judge, Dominick A. Hall, dismissed the suit. He stated that since neither Livingston nor Shreve were residents of Louisiana the case was invalid. Thus, the monopoly was broken on the Mississippi and the river opened to competitive steamboat development five years before the Livingston-Fulton monopoly ended in the East.

Shreve had been a popular figure on the river. Now, because of his stand against the monopolists his popularity increased, especially since he was also acclaimed for having demonstrated the practicability of navigation far up the river. He went on to improve his steamboats, building others such as the *Post Boy* in 1819, the first river steamer to carry mail in the West. In 1827 President John Quincy Adams appointed him Superintendent of Western River Improvements, a position he held until 1841.

In 1829 Shreve designed and built a steamboat called the *Heliopolis* (City of the Sun), the first steam "snagboat." Called "Uncle Sam's toothpuller," it pulled or drew sunken tree trunks from the river. (Snags are branches of great trees, or the trees themselves, which are torn out along the banks and carried along by the floods until they are covered with sand and remain fixed with one end directed upward, creating a danger to navigation.) Such snagboats helped clear the river of many of these obstructions which were always a menace to river traffic. In the 1830s, using snagboats of this kind, Shreve cleared the Red River of a gigantic floating raft—a driftwood jam about 160 miles long. The jam had been building for centuries, and through those years had become a vast island. The Red River jam had prevented upriver traffic from passing northward, impeding the development of northern Louisiana, Texas, and Oklahoma along the river. The camp Shreve set up for this job grew so large that it was incorporated in 1839 under the name Shreveport.

In 1815, after his first trip up the Mississippi to Louisville, Shreve had predicted that soon the trip would be made in as short a time as ten days. His prediction was an accurate one, and by 1825 some steamboats were covering the distance in as little as six days. Soon many steamboats were racing along at fourteen or sixteen miles an hour. While this enabled them to cover the distance in a little over three days, the time was lengthened due to the necessity of making stops for freight, passengers, and fuel.

Even at this slow pace, travel by steamboat in the early days was a far cry from the days when upriver travel went along at a mile an hour. Still, because of the enormous amount of river traffic and freight, keelboats and barges did not suddenly disappear. In 1826 the average number of steamboats arriving at Pittsburgh each month was six; the average number of keelboats and canal boats

A contemporary pencil sketch of a small early western steamboat.

was thirty-nine. Keelboats were still being used at the mid-century, but the averages were quite different. By the 1850s the monthly arrivals of steamboats at Pittsburgh were two hundred and sixty-five; for keelboats and canal boats the average was forty-nine.

As had been foreseen early in the history of steamers, freight rates dropped, and as their use increased the drop became greater. In 1815 the shipment of a barrel of flour going from Cincinnati to New Orleans cost $1.50; in the years after 1840 when the surge in steamboat building increased, the rate for a barrel of flour over the same route went down to an average of only fifty cents, and in some years it went as low as twenty-five cents.

With the building of so many steamboats, engine shops and foundries were established. Urban areas developed around new plants for meat packing, flour milling, glass manufacturing, and the manufacture of other goods. Skilled and unskilled workers, as well as farmers settling new areas away from the river centers, found work. Not only emigrants from the eastern seaboard, but those traveling across the Atlantic from Europe found the area increasingly promising. A farmer from Germany arriving at New York could go up the Hudson in a steamboat and across New York State from Albany to Buffalo on the Erie Canal; then by steamboat out of Buffalo he headed farther west to Detroit or Chicago. The cities of the West grew rapidly: Chicago had a population of one hundred fifty people in 1832 (New York City, that is Manhattan, had well over 200,000 citizens at that time); by 1850 Chicago held over twenty-nine thousand people.

CHAPTER 6

Later Steamboat Development in the West

SOME EARLY steamboats were elegant, both in the East and the West, but they were outnumbered by those that were only moderately equipped and often poorly operated. In the early days the Mississippi boats were generally unsatisfactory vehicles for passengers because they were built mainly to carry freight. One early small Mississippi steamer was described as slow, unstable, and like a fiery furnace. On another the cabin was "Small, dirty, crowded, close, and smokey."

The *General Pike*, built in 1818, was the first steamer in the West constructed for passenger service alone. The apartments aboard were said to be spacious and superbly furnished, the cabins large and comfortable, and the fourteen staterooms decorated in the highest style. But steamers such as this were not the rule, they were the exception.

An interesting feature of the *General Pike* was

that it is said to have drawn only three feet three inches of water when unloaded. Some steamboats before this date drew less water. The Livingston-Fulton *Buffalo* of 1814 drew only two and a half feet unloaded and as much as five feet loaded. Still, this was an unusual draft for large steamboats even as late as the 1840s. Boats with a draft of six to eight feet could easily manage most of the Mississippi, as well as a fair way up the branches of the river.

In later years many steamboats, especially the smaller western ones, developed shallower, broader holds than the earlier boats; but the holds of large vessels were six feet deep or over. In 1850 Frederick Law Olmsted, discussing the steamboats on the Cape Fear River, wrote: "In summer, there are sometimes but eighteen inches of water on the bars: the boat I was in drew but fourteen inches, light [unloaded]. She was a stern-wheel craft—the boiler and engine [high pressure] being placed at opposite ends, to balance weights. Her burden was three hundred barrels, or sixty tons measurement. This is the character of most of the boats navigating the river—of which there are now twelve. Larger boats are almost useless in summer, from their liability to ground; and even smaller ones, at low stages of water, carry no freight, but are employed to tow up 'flats' or shallow barges."

The *Yorktown*, built in 1844, had a hold eight feet in depth, yet she drew only four feet of water light, and barely over eight feet when loaded with 500 tons of freight. It was not uncommon for these boats to be so heavily loaded that the deck guards were in the river with water washing over them, giving them the appearance of being flush on the water and not in it, but this appearance was a deception.

The hull design of river boats on American rivers did change slowly and with a curious twist: in the East they were at first shallow, long, and narrow—and flat bottomed. The very first Livingston-Fulton boat built in Paris in 1803 was flat bottomed, as were their later boats until 1815 in the East. Other eastern boats such as Oliver Evans's of 1804 were also flat. With the building of the *Fulton*, designed to run on Long Island Sound, they began to be constructed with round bottoms, like ships.

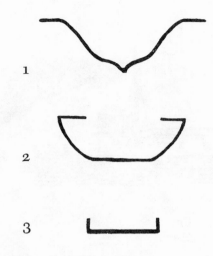

Three different types of steamer hull design: (1) the ship body, (2) the flat-bottomed rounded hull, and (3) the flat-bottomed boat.

In the West, steamboats were built along conventional ship lines at first and developed a shallow hull slowly in the larger boats. As the steamboat ventured farther up the branches of the Mississippi they had to be shallow-draft boats to operate in places where the water was extremely low. In the later years flat-bottomed boats with stern wheels were common in the West, but these were not the vessels usually used for travel. Flat-bottomed boats appeared all through the West. The *Explorer*, the first steamboat to appear on the

The Western Engineer *was the first steamer to ascend the Missouri River.*

Colorado in 1858, was a scow (a flat-bottomed vessel used as a freight carrier): it was much like a pointed flatboat with sides. Many steam ferries also had flat bottoms: they were actually rafts with paddle wheels attached. All these flat boats when not loaded with freight drew about two feet of water. In the early years, vessels of any size, used either for freight or passenger service, had holds and their hulls were ship-like.

This is contrary to the popular belief that one day in 1816 Henry Shreve developed the "flat"-hulled, many-decked Mississippi steamboat. From then on, *all* western steamers are supposed to have

been similar to overgrown flatboats: they were supposed to run "*on* the water instead of in it." (They were said to have been so flat and ride so high that they could navigate on a heavy dew.) But Shreve's boat the *Washington* had a keel, a hold, and enough room in the hold to house the engine. The tales of large Mississippi steamers floating easily over sandbars a few inches below the surface are myths: considering the elaborate mechanism the larger steamers carried (an arrangement of poles and jacks) to get them off sandbars and out of low-water regions they so often got stuck in, it is a wonder that they were ever thought to be as shallow-draft as is so often assumed. As for Shreve, he probably would be remembered for his many fine achievements that were real if people did not so often dwell on his "flat-bottomed" boat. But in later vessels, the keel was internal and the bottom was truly flat.

The *Western Engineer*, one of the steamboats used on the Yellowstone Expedition in 1819, had a draft of only nineteen inches, light. It was built under the direction of Major Stephen H. Long, of the United States Topographical Engineers, especially for use on this expedition to construct forts and discover, if possible, the source of the Missouri River. It was built near Pittsburgh in 1818; the *New York Commercial Advertiser* described it as being "well armed, and carries an elegant flag painted by Mr. [Titian R.] Peale [who accompanied the expedition] representing a white man and an Indian shaking hands, the Calumet [tobacco-pipe] of peace and a sword. The boat is seventy-five feet long, thirteen feet beam, draws nineteen inches of water with her engine which, together with all the machinery is placed below deck entirely out of sight. The steam passes off through the mouth of the figure-head, a large serpent. The wheels are placed in the stern, to avoid the snags and sawyers [a rocking snag] which are so common in these waters."

Despite the fact that it drew so little water when not loaded, the *Western Engineer* was not a success on the expedition. But, of the four steamboats that were used, it worked its way farthest upriver, to Council Bluffs about six hundred and fifty miles from St. Louis. The river was low and the *Western Engineer,* with Long as navigator, continually ran aground. It carried a heavy load of supplies, sat low in the water, and its engine was weak as all early steamboat engines were: it was necessary to tow it across sandbars and through the swift main currents. The boilers clogged with sediment and the boat had to be stopped, the boilers cooled, then cleaned and reheated—often a number of times a day.

Although the small- and medium-sized shallow-draft steamers dominated western and southern rivers, they were not glorified in song and story as were the large, elaborately decorated river passenger boats of the southern Mississippi. (The large passenger vessels operating on the northern Mississippi were handsome, clean, and attractively furnished, but not ostentatious or flamboyant as the boats in the lower river were in the later days.) Yet the smaller steamers were greatly responsible for the West's rapid development. They serviced the river settlements by the thousands, and long lines of steamers, belching clouds of black smoke, were to be seen strung along the banks of American rivers for many, many years.

Taking a trip on a medium-sized steamer on the Mississippi, a passenger wrote: "They are but scows in build, perfectly flat, with pointed stem and square stern. Behind is one small wheel, moved by two small engines of the simplest and cheapest construction. Drawing but a foot of water [light] they keep afloat in the lowest stages of the rivers. Their freight, wood, machinery, hands and steerage passengers are all on the main deck. Eight or ten feet above, supported by light stanchions is the floor used by the passengers, one long saloon 8 or 10 feet wide which stretches from the stern to the smoke pipes far forward . . . The

Examples of small, medium and large steamers of the West.

perils and annoyances connected with this mode of transportation became apparent when we struck a snag and broke several buckets of the wheel. After being partially repaired the boat frequently grounded, and, although it was always released after more or less delay, it was at last driven hard and fast by rapids upon a heap of rocks barely covered by water."

The smaller steamers in comparison to the larger passenger boats are almost always described as crowded, poorly constructed, and unsanitary vessels. They had small portholes all around that barely admitted light and air. The engine was more often than not in the cabin with the bunks when there was no second deck, and the bunks were uncomfortable and often shared with rats. There were seldom any provisions for washing, and toilets were simple boxes sticking out over the water, often built inside the paddle box.

In the South and on much of the Mississippi the hands working on the boat were often slaves rented or owned by the captain, and if not, immigrants from Europe, especially the Irish who were usually given the heavy and dangerous work to do. Slaves were expensive property, fairly well treated in an offhand manner, and often protected from risk at the expense of the immigrant. If an Irish or German worker, newly arrived in the country, was killed or injured another quickly took his place.

Navigational directions for guiding vessels up

and down the Mississippi and other rivers appeared in the form of such works as Samuel Cuming's *The Western Pilot*, published in Cincinnati in 1839. It consisted of detailed charts and directions for use of these charts in following the course of the river from Pittsburgh to New Orleans. The directions for Map No. 1, for the Ohio River, began: "From the landing at Pittsburgh, on the Monongahela side, keep near the right shore, and, at high water, pull directly out into the Allegheny current which sets strong over to the left shore. At low water, when nearly up to the point, keep over to the left, towards O'Hara's glass works, which will carry you clear of the bar at the point, and of the Monongahela bar on the left." Then in bold print: "Brunot's Island," with the indication that this island is two and a half miles below Pittsburgh. Then it gives directions to the next island, five miles farther down, and then covers the next nine and a half miles to Dead

Map No. 1 from Cuming's The Western Pilot. *The directions, quoted in the text, begin: "From the landing at Pittsburgh, on the Monongahela side, keep near the right shore . . ." The line down the middle of the river is the route a river pilot was to follow to ply the river safely.*

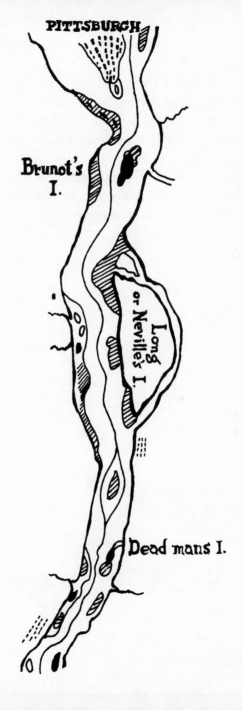

PITTSBURGH

Brunot's I.

Long or Neville's I.

Dead mans I.

Man's Island. Charts and navigational directions of this kind had been in use for thousands of years.

The pilot guides used in the West were heavily laden with the latest information concerning the changes in the river's course and such additional information as the disappearance of islands. They were dotted with references to artificial channels and shifting bars, and when passing a bluff told the pilot how many yards to stand clear in order to be carried safely past. Their main omission, of necessity, was the indication of where snags under the water would be: snags caused most of the damage to both steamboats and flatboats. Damage by snags on the Ohio and Mississippi between the years of 1822 and 1832 is estimated to have been nearly $2,000,000 through loss of vessels and cargoes.

CHAPTER 7

Steamboats on the Lakes and Bays of America

THE INTRODUCTION of steamboats on the lakes of America began on the quiet waters of Lake Champlain. The first lake steamboat was the *Vermont,* built by John and James Winans in 1808–09. The *Vermont* traveled the one hundred twenty miles between Whitehall, New York, and St. Johns, Quebec. An insight into the accommodations and conditions aboard the *Vermont* and other early steamers is given by the set of regulations passengers were supposed to follow. These regulations were posted aboard ship and read: "As the time at which the boat may arrive at the different places may vary a few hours, according to the advantage or disadvantage of the wind, those wishing to come on board will see the necessity of being on the spot two hours before" the boat was scheduled to leave. It goes on: "Passengers will breakfast before they come on board; dinner will be served up exactly at 2 o'clock; tea, with meats, which is also supper, at eight in the evening, and breakfast at seven in the morning. No one has a claim on the steward for victuals at any other hours. One dollar to be paid for each dog or animal. No horses taken on board; as, if they were about too much, there is difficulty in steering the boat.

"The back cabin of twelve berths which will accommodate sixteen persons, is exclusively for the ladies and their children. Servants to sleep on the floor. Any greater number of persons, who pay full fare, will be accommodated with sofas or cross-lockers."

The cabin for the men could accommodate twenty-four persons, all under strict obligation not to "smoke in the ladies' cabin or in the great cabin under the penalty, first, of one dollar and a half, and a half a dollar for each half hour they offend against the rule; the money to be spent in wine for the company." There was a similar penalty for anyone lying down in a berth with his boots or shoes on.

The first regulation is interesting because it mentions the advantages of wind to early steamboats. These early steamers carried sail, as did the first steamships that crossed the Atlantic. Sometimes the reason for the use of sail is simply stated: "sail was used when the unreliable engine broke down." That engines broke down now and then is true; but sail had other uses on steamboats and steamships.

The sails were used when the engine was cleaned, and this took place often, for deposits in the boiler prevented steam from being produced, especially at sea. Sail was also used at times when the engine was in perfect operation in order to gain speed. Then, too, as D. T. Valentine explains in his steamboat manual of 1852: "Steamboats on the North River first performed their trips with wood. Lackawanna coal was afterward introduced, by which the expense of fuel was reduced from $150 a day to $50." All American steamboats at first used wood for fuel, and when the fuel ran out, the sails were hoisted. Sails were never used to any extent on the Mississippi system however, for the current was too fast and the river too crooked.

The fuel-carrying capacity of a steamboat or ship was not great. Wood-burning steamboats had to make frequent stops to take on fuel. To keep up pressure the boiler had to be fed wood at a hurried and continual pace. Fueling stations were set up along the river in clearings to which wood cutters would bring wood for storage and sale. To save on fuel during times when the wind was favorable the sail was unfurled and the vessel proceeded under sail.

The *New Orleans* and other western steamers used sails, but they were given up when western steamers began to be constructed with many decks. It is not a simple matter to foot a mast in a vessel with three high decks and a shallow hold. It would not have been much use, anyway, for the sail area would be small compared to the size of the vessel and would do little to move the boat against the current, especially if the vessel carried a heavy freight load.

To get fuel, the steamboat would be run ashore at points where wood was stored for sale; then deck hands worked frantically in gangs to get the wood aboard as fast as possible so as not to delay the trip. Passengers could help—if they did they sometimes received a discount on their fare. (Many times impatient passengers pitched in and helped load the wood simply to get the steamer on the move again.)

A good description of "wooding up" is given by a passenger on a small early steamer: "Soon after leaving, we passed the *Zephyr,* wooding up: an hour later, our own boat was run to the bank, men jumped from her fore and aft, and fastened head and stern lines to the trees, and we also commenced wooding.

"The trees had been cut away so as to leave a clear space to the top of the bank, which was some fifty feet from the boat, and moderately steep. Wood, cut, split, and piled in ranks, stood at the top of it, and a chute of plank, two feet wide and thirty long, conveyed it nearly to the water. The crew rushed to the wood-piles—master, passengers, and all, but the engineer and chambermaid, deserting the boat—and the wood was first passed down, as many as could, throwing into the chute, and others forming a line, and tossing it, from one to another, down the bank. From the water's edge it was passed, in the same way, to its place on board, with great rapidity—the crew exciting themselves with yells . . ." This wood cost $1.75 a cord: a cord of wood is eight feet long, four feet high and four feet wide.

Another method of fueling was by wood-carrying flatboats that tied up to the steamboat; the logs were thrown aboard as the steamer continued on its way. This operation was supposedly so fast that Mark Twain said the wood would be loaded before you could wipe your eyeglasses.

Even with these fueling methods engineers sometimes ran out of fuel; on the Mississippi, where sail was not often used even in the early days, barrels, spars, and floor planks were torn up to keep the fire going until the next fuel stop, or the boat landed and wood was cut. The cutting of wood was common on early steamers, for there were not as yet the number of fueling stops that appeared later. One steamboat hand wrote: "At first we could buy our fire wood, but higher up [the river] we could not do so. Every evening we had to get out and cut it ourselves." Some steamboats still used wood for fuel right into the 1900s.

After the *Vermont,* the next steamboat put under construction was the *Ticonderoga* on Lake Champlain. But Commodore Thomas Macdonough, who was in charge of American forces on that lake during the War of 1812, seized it before it was completed, and it was converted into a schooner. When the war ended a second steamboat was launched and put into service on Champlain. This was the *Phoenix,* constructed by Captain J. Sherman in 1815. (*Phoenix, Comet, Enterprise, Fulton*—and many other common names—were used to designate a number of different steamboats and sailing craft.)

The *Vermont* and the *Phoenix* traveled both day and night to accomplish the one-hundred-twenty-mile trip between New York State and Canada in twenty-four hours. It is during the night of September 5, 1819, that there occurred one of the first steamboat fires. Such fires, along with explosions, plagued steamboat travel through the years. In this case the captain of the *Phoenix,* a young man of twenty-two named Richard Sherman, saved all aboard. "The passengers rushed in crowds upon the deck and attempted to seize the small boats. They were met by the Captain, who having aban-

The Walk in the Water, *one of the first steamers on the upper Great Lakes.*

doned hope of saving his boat, now thought only of saving his passengers, and stood by the gangway with a pistol in each hand, determined to prevent any person from jumping into the boats before they were properly lowered into the water." Captain Sherman did not leave the burning wreck until he was certain everyone aboard the steamboat was safely ashore.

Progress was taking place in establishing steamboats on the Great Lakes also, but it was slow. These bodies of water are treacherous, even for sailing vessels. The Great Lakes are rough, unpredictable inland seas of enormous depth and area. They cover 96,000 square miles and stretch 1,555 miles in length. Their surface is often, in the space of a half hour, turned from a smooth, calm body of water into a roaring sea with destructive twenty-five-foot waves.

The *Walk in the Water* built by Noah Brown at Black Rock (Buffalo, New York) in 1818 is often cited as the first successful steamboat on the Great Lakes, but many newspapers and magazines of the early 1800s give quite a different picture of the situation. A report in the *Merchant Magazine and Commercial Review* of 1847 presents one of the best and briefest histories of early steam vessels on the Great Lakes. This history agrees with many existing reports in American and Canadian newspapers printed in the years 1816, 1817, and 1818. It is given here because it is so informative and concise. The report reads: "The editors of the *Commercial Times,* published at Oswego, one of the principal ports on Lake Ontario, furnish us with the following brief history of the progress of steam navigation on that Lake:—

"The rapid increase and general improvement in the commercial marine of the Lakes, impart a high degree of interest of everything relating to the early history and progress of our steam navigation. We have therefore collected the facts and compiled the following table, showing the names, tonnage and captains of all the American steamers which have navigated Lake Ontario since the first introduction of steam here, in 1816. In that year the first steamboat, the *Ontario,* was built at Sackett's Harbor, and commenced running in the spring of 1817. She was the first steamer built on the Western Lakes, and ran from Ogdensburgh to Lewiston, making the trip in ten days, charging $15 for cabin passage, and continued to run until the year 1831. Her engine was made by Mr. J. P. Allaire, of the city of New York. Gen. Jacob Brown, Com. M. T. Woolsey, Hooker & Crane, Charles Smyth, Erie Lusher, and Elisha Camp, were the proprietors of the *Ontario.* Her construction as the first vessel propelled by steam built

West of the Hudson [in New York]; and the first sea vessel of the kind we believe ever built in this country, was considered an experiment and an enterprise, at the time, of the first magnitude. She left Sackett's Harbor early in the spring of 1817 on her first trip, and reached Oswego the same day, where she was received by the people with extravagant demonstrations—such as the firing of cannon and most enthusiastic greetings. Many of the people of Oswego continued their rejoicing all night and till the boat left the next day. It was a wonderful occasion, one that commanded the admiration and engrossed the attention of the people.

"On the morning of the second day of her trip the *Ontario* left Oswego and reached Genesee River in the evening, where she remained till the next day, when she proceeded on her way up the Lake. Soon after leaving the river, she encountered a Northeast blow, which raised a considerable sea. Like all steamers previously built, her shaft, on which the wheels revolved, was confined to the boxes in which it ran by its own weight, only. The action of the sea upon her wheels soon lifted the shaft from its bed, so that the wheelhouses were instantly torn to pieces, utterly demolished by the wheels, with a tremendous crash, doing considerable damage to the wheels. Upon this disaster, the steamer put about; and, with the aid of canvas, returned to Sackett's Harbor to repair damages and secure her shaft.

"The next steamer on Lake Ontario was built by the Canadians in 1817, and was called the *Frontenac*. She was a vessel of 70 tons, and had her engine imported from England.

"The *Sophia*, of 75 tons, was built at Sackett's Harbor in 1818, to run between that place and Kingston. In the same year the first steamer on Lake Erie, the *Walk in the Water*, was built. In 1823 the *Martha Ogden* was built at Sackett's Harbor, under the direction and control of the late Albert Crane, Esq., of Oswego, which, in connection with the *Ontario*, formed the line of American steamers for many years, down to 1830, to which time lake steamers were considered an experiment. They had no regular day for leaving port, but made their trips conform to the appearance of the weather. The boat building at French Creek for the Ontario Company, nearly ready to launch, will be much superior in dimensions and style of fitting up to any boat on the lake."

The unusual name given the *Walk in the Water* may have been one of the reasons it has taken precedence over the *Ontario, Frontenac,* and *Sophia* for so long in so many histories of steamboating; it has a sort of glamour that once appealed to many Americans influenced by Longfellow's *The Song of Hiawatha*. Another reason the *Ontario* was omitted from many histories was that in the late 1800s the story began to circulate that the vessel had been so damaged on its first voyage that it never operated on the Lakes, although the story is not true.

The engine for the *Walk in the Water* was, as were other U.S. Lake steamer engines, made in New York City. It went by sloop up to Albany, then overland in wagons to Buffalo: this trip took nearly a month. Captain John Fish piloted the *Walk in the Water* on its first voyage that began at Buffalo on August 23, 1818. The steamboat arrived in Cleveland on the 25th, and as usual when steamboat service was introduced at that time, the people of Cleveland gave the vessel a roaring welcome. On the 28th the steamer reached its destination at Detroit.

There were hundreds of people to greet the boat at Detroit, among them many Indians. At first, steamboats were such an alien type of vessel to the Indians that they were invariably frightened by them; they either fled in terror, or boldly attempted to attack the smoking, clanking boat. Often Indians, like uninformed whites, believed steamboats were sea monsters come to destroy them. A good part of their fear was provoked because they did not understand how a vessel could move without being poled or paddled.

Before the *Walk in the Water* arrived on the

Detroit River, the settlers told the Indians that a great ship was coming. They mentioned that they, the settlers, were so powerful that even the fish in the Lakes obeyed them—therefore the new boat would be drawn by a school of sturgeons. The Indians cried out in amazement when the steamboat arrived, believing the incredible story they had been told. This bit of frontier humor, true or not, points up the technological gap between the two groups that was so heavily in favor of the settlers.

Although many Indians continued to fear and dislike steamboats, some were not in the least fearful once the mode of operation was explained. In 1823, when the *Virginia* undertook a voyage from St. Louis to Fort Snelling with soap, candles, powder, ammunition, and other supplies, a Sauk chief, Great Eagle, was aboard with two of his children. When the *Virginia* went aground on a bar that the chief had warned the pilot about, he became impatient with such stupidity and slowness, so he dove over the side, and with his children following swam ashore. When the steamboat arrived at Fort Edwards the next day Great Eagle was already there.

The operator of the *Walk in the Water*, as those of the earlier steamers on Champlain and the Great Lakes, paid the Livingston-Fulton company for the privilege of running their steamboats. It carried two masts and the paddle wheels were sixteen feet in diameter. In still waters it could make nearly eight miles an hour (the rate of speed for steamboats on rivers was never given in nautical knots), but often the vessel had to be drawn by oxen for considerable distance when leaving or entering Buffalo because of the strong current in the harbor. The usual time for the Buffalo-Detroit run was three days and cost eighteen dollars; the same voyage usually took a week or two by sailboat.

An early steam ferry in the Great Lakes region.

The *Walk in the Water* was wrecked in a storm near Buffalo in October of 1821. The engine was taken out and put into another Lake steamer, the *Superior*, in 1822. During the three years the *Walk in the Water* operated, it paid only one dividend to its owners. The *Superior* had a similar poor financial record and was soon converted to a sloop-rigged sailing ship for carrying lumber. The spread of steam navigation on the Lakes was slow. By 1831 there were only eleven steamboats operating. Sailing vessels held a great lead until the locks and canals connecting the Lakes were constructed. Steamboats could navigate the locks and narrow connecting waterways with ease, while it was difficult for the sailing vessels to get through without grounding and other accidents, so the steamers gradually took the lead.

By the late 1840s a Norwegian lawyer, Ole Munch Ræder, visiting the United States to study the American jury system, was able to state: "On the Great Lakes there is only one means of travel, for immigrants as well as for others, and that is the steamship. The elegance of such a ship is quite remarkable. The vessel is equipped in every possible way for the convenience of the passengers; there is, for example, a barber shop. There is also a band." He went on to say that the band was not very good, but the dancing was "dainty." There was also a piano aboard, and it appeared "strange to see how easy it was to induce these American ladies, noted in Europe for their prudery and finicality [over-niceness], to play or sing for this audience of absolute strangers from every corner of the earth."

Besides the lakes, the enormous bays of America were also becoming sailing waters for steamers. One of the first introduced on Chesapeake Bay was the *Eagle*. It was twenty-two feet wide and one hundred thirty feet long with an average speed of about five miles an hour. Steamboats were popular on Chesapeake Bay for travel to the eastern shore of Maryland, Virginia, and by a common means of interrupted steamer-stage travel, to Philadelphia. In a book printed in 1826 by an anonymous Alabama man who called himself simply a "Traveller" a vivid picture of steamboat-stagecoach travel during the early years of steamboating is presented.

The writer begins: "*Journey to Philadelphia.*— We left Baltimore about sun-down, and arrived in Philadelphia about sun-rise next morning . . . the distance between ninety and a hundred miles; fare $4. This journey is performed partly by steamboats and partly by stages. You leave Baltimore in a steam-boat, and sailing down Patapsco [River], land at Frenchtown. Here you take the stage to

Newcastle (Delaware,) and then take the steam-boat again, and sailing up the Delaware, arrive at Philadelphia. It is very unpleasant to those who wish to see the country, to make this journey in the night: to me, it was provoking; nor can I see through the policy of such a plan, which deprives the traveller of so much pleasure. The night was dark and dismal, so much so, that it precluded the view of every object.

"The steam-boats in these waters, are elegantly furnished with every article of convenience, particularly in the articles of meat and drink (though gentlemen and ladies breakfast, dine, and sup together) [segregation of the sexes was the rule on Southern steamers, and on early Mississippi steamers during meals: in the North men and women shared their meals from the beginning of steamboating] yet they are greatly inferior in size, to the steam-boats in the western rivers: the ball-room in the General Green is fully as long as most of the boats in these rivers. [He had not yet seen the Hudson steamers; when he did he admired them greatly and was impressed by their size.] Nor is the furniture equal to ours; I have seen no satin spreads, or gold fringe in any of them as yet, which are common in our boats, although we are looked upon as little more than savages, by many of the people in these large cities. Here, as well as there, you must choose your birth, and have it registered, or go without, as was the case with many of us to night, the passengers exceeding the number of births. I richly deserved my fate, as I was the first on board, and neglecting to engage one, had to sit up . . .

"About midnight we came to shore, and here was pulling, hauling, settling bills and fare. An hundred people were in motion, men, women, children, and parrots. Here was every one running to get their ticket: 'I want my ticket, give me my ticket:' they overset me several times. In short, being at a loss to comprehend the meaning of the ticket, and thinking I might in some way be concerned, I brushed the dust from my clothes as well as I could, made up to my friend of Baltimore, and asked her the meaning." He had, now, to buy his ticket for the stagecoach; when he got the ticket he raced to get a seat, and, "Nothing could equal the uproar and confusion which now took place; such running with porters, band-boxes, trunks, and portmanteaus, flying in all directions; such pushing, elbowing, and trampling on one's toes; it was emphatically every one for himself." He finally settled in his coach, and: "The cavalcade now set forward, in a solemn walk, without one lamp amongst seven or eight, perhaps ten stages. . . It seemed an age before we arrived at

Newcastle, and here we had to get out in the dark, and grope our way to the steam-boat, which we did not quit till we landed at Philadelphia."

It does not sound as if this "traveller" enjoyed his journey. As we shall see, many others shared similar discomforts for the sake of traveling at night and attending to business or personal matters during the day. An interesting point about this gentleman is that he tells us he had never seen a sailing ship before he took this trip and was much impressed by the first one he came across at the coast. But, when it came to steamboats he had seen many of them in Alabama and the West, for by the late 1820s there was not a river settlement that did not try to possess one of these mechanical craft. In places where the river was too low to support a steamer the citizens bemoaned the fact that without one their section of the river would never be able to grow, and more often than not such was the case.

CHAPTER 8

Steamboats in Europe

THE ADVANTAGES of the steamboat over sailing vessels on rivers and lakes were clearly understood in America, and during the early 1800s many steamers were built and put to work hauling passengers and freight over long distances. Although the usefulness of steam navigation was also obvious to many Europeans, there were a number of reasons steamboats were not so widely adopted in Europe at first. The geographical makeup of areas in Europe where industry was evolving, and where steamboats would best be put to use, was not favorable. Lacking a network of rivers covering thousands of miles, such as those in the United States, steamboats were used as ferries and in coastal trade, as well as for short voyages at sea. Confined, as it almost completely was, to ferry and coastal service, steamboat development was not rapid. Voyages at sea for which the industrial countries of Europe later used the steamship were not practical because steam-driven vessels could not cover long distances without being refueled a number of times.

In addition, the industrial countries were at war during much of the late eighteenth century and early nineteenth century. When periods of peace finally did come, industrialization forced European governments and individuals to use money to develop factories and such internal improvements as railways, rather than encouraging shipping.

In the late 1830s and early '40s, European industries felt an urgent demand for raw materials. It was only then that steam navigation became an important factor in many European countries. Americans used the steamboat to exploit and settle vast unoccupied areas—Europeans, already settled and with fairly well established national boundaries, used the steamboat to carry large quantities of foodstuffs for the rapidly growing population, raw materials for factories, and for exporting manufactured goods. By the 1840s and 1850s steam navigation was wholeheartedly adopted in Europe.

It was not until steamships were able to cross the oceans of the world efficiently that Europeans displayed their talent in building steamers. Still, early in the 1800s, there were many men in Europe who saw great possibilities in steam navigation. As we have seen, the French were intrigued with the steamboat's possibilities very early, as were

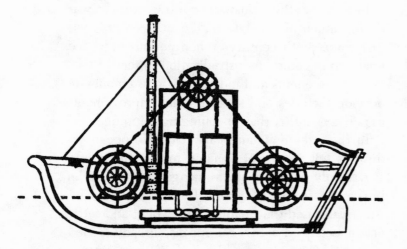

Diagram of Patrick Miller's catamaran with William Symington's engine.

the English, but it was in Scotland that the first practical steamboats came into existence.

On October 14, 1788, a small steamboat of unusual design was going through trials on a lake at Dalswinton, Scotland. The designer of this novel craft was Patrick Miller, an Edinburgh banker. Miller had been experimenting with mechanical boats for a number of years and had already designed and operated a boat with two hulls (a catamaran) between which he set five paddle wheels. This craft at first was operated by men; then, using only two paddle wheels, it was driven by an engine designed by William Symington.

Symington's engine worked on the atmospheric principle, as Newcomen's did, but it included a separate condenser, which was an infringement on Watt's patent. In the spring of 1790 Symington was prevented from further experiments until Watt's patent expired in 1800. Then there was a rush at the patent office and among the petitions was one submitted by Symington for a paddle wheel drive arrangement worked by his engine and fitted into a steam tug.

Symington's arrangement was put into the stern of a small boat a little over fifty feet long. The boat had been ordered by Lord Dundas and was named after his daughter Charlotte. In the spring of 1802 it towed two barges for about twenty

The Charlotte Dundas, *successful during its trial run, was nevertheless tied up and left to rot.*

miles on the Forth-Clyde Canal. The men who worked on the canal were very much against the use of the mechanical boat; it was also believed that the waves created by the *Charlotte Dundas* would eat away the canal's bank and cause expensive upkeep; therefore the steamboat was tied up and left to rot. Both of these boats were successful, but neither was ever used outside its trial run. Like many of the early experimenters before him, Symington died in poverty.

At the time no one thought much of the Miller or Dundas boats, and it was not until after Fulton's success on the Hudson that a practical steamboat appeared in Europe: this also occurred in Scotland. The boat appeared in 1812 and was named the *Comet*. It was designed and operated by Henry Bell, a determined steamboat enthusiast. As early as 1803 Bell attempted to interest naval men in steam navigation, but the navy was not interested in steamers for a number of reasons. Navy men considered steamboats dirty because of the soot. They were used to clean sailing vessels. At least the decks were clean—when the first bathroom was introduced very late in the 1800s this conversation was reported:

First Sea Lord, Sir Alexander Milne, "Did you ever wash when you went to sea?"
Sir Sidney Dacres, answered: "No."
"No more did I," replied the First Sea Lord, scandalized by the innovation.

Then too, steamboats were considered unsafe at sea because of the risk of fire aboard a wooden vessel. Steamers also had a very short range because of their need to be refueled. And while steamers had more maneuverability, one lucky shot by the enemy could disable its paddle wheel or engine and leave the ship helpless. The Admiralty was not impressed with Bell's suggestion.

Steam was slowly adopted by the navies of the world only when screw propellers took the place of paddle wheels, iron replaced wood in hulls, and engines were more efficient and powerful.

Bell had already begun experimenting as early as 1800 when he installed a boiler and engine in a small boat. His main problem, like Fitch's, was money. He was not wealthy, nor did he have a wealthy backer, as Hulls had had in England earlier. Bell had been a carpenter and bricklayer and had also served as an apprentice in a shipyard. He opened a small hotel in Helensburg, Scotland, and eventually accumulated enough money to put his ideas about steamers to work.

The separate sections of the *Comet* that made it a steamboat were not designed by Bell. The hull was ordered in October of 1811 from the Port Glasgow shipyard of John Wood & Sons; the boiler was constructed by John Napier and Sons; and the engine was designed by John Robertson of Glasgow. This engine was a modified Watt beam engine—the name "beam engine" came into use with the building of the huge Newcomen engines (some as tall as a three-story building) with a twenty-five-foot-long oak beam pivoted at the center and rocking up and down like a giant seasaw. The wooden beam was later replaced by a huge metal arm, although the engine was still called a beam engine.

The *Comet* was launched on July 24, 1812, and a few days later steamed from Port Glasgow to Glasgow a few miles away. An advertisement on August 14 announced that the steamboat would ply between Glasgow, Greenock, and Helensburgh (the complete round-trip covering just over 40 miles). The advertisement also mentioned that the boat would travel "by air, wind and steam." There was a sail hung on the funnel, and no mast was used: this at first, was to be a peculiarity on a number of European steamboats.

The *Comet* was originally a sidewheeler with two wheels on each side, but this was not an efficient arrangement, so Bell converted the vessel to a single wheel on each side. The run between Glasgow and Helensburgh was not a success although Bell tried a number of novel approaches such as having a small band to entertain the passengers, a feature later adopted by many steamboat lines. In 1813 Bell put the *Comet* into coastal service, where it was much more successful and operated for ten years until it was wrecked.

In 1813 another steamboat, the *Charlotte*, appeared in Europe, this time in England, plying the Avon River between Bristol and Bath. It carried about thirty cabin passengers and a number of "steerage" passengers. "Steerage" was the part of the vessel allotted to passengers who paid the cheapest rate; it originally meant the steerage cabin, or the place from which the ship was steered. It was in the afterpart of the vessel in front of the main cabin, that is the second cabin. Later the term came to mean, generally, anyplace aboard a vessel that was set aside for passengers paying the least amount of money for passage. The *Charlotte* was built by a lawyer, Theodore Lawrance, and was not successful at first. It was taken out of service and improvements were made in the engine as well as in the vessel itself.

The faster, roomier, and more comfortable *Charlotte* was commented on in a Bristol newspaper. "It was truly pleasing to see the ease and dexterity with which it handled. It was several times put about in a space scarcely more than its own length, and so very easily that no idea can be entertained of difficulty in avoiding loaded vessels, or other impediments on the river; and from its peculiar construction the velocity of it can be stopped almost in an instant." The improved vessel was not much more successful, however. The Bristol to Bath run was cut from daily runs to three times a week, then in 1814 discontinued completely.

Nowhere was the steamboat's arrival greeted with cheers by the men who worked on sailing craft: they saw it as a threat that endangered their livelihood. River men in general disliked the steamboat with such vehemence that they often crashed head-on into powered vessels with their sailing craft. When the wind was in its favor a sailing vessel could thunder into a steamboat with a great deal of force and cause much damage to the vessel and injury to those aboard. River men soon learned that the most vulnerable section of a steamer was its paddle wheels and "accidents" often occurred, with the paddle as the prime target. Of course some accidents between the two different types of vessels were unintentional, but the result was the same, and damage to the wheel or hull put a steamboat out of operation until repairs were made. That the *Charlotte* could put about several times in a space scarcely more than its own length no doubt came in handy when the captain wanted to avoid collision.

Often on these early steamboats the passengers, regardless of risk, gathered on deck "to see the smash." Despite the fact that these encounters between sail and steam offered entertainment to the paying customers, steamboat operators lost no time in covering the paddle wheels with heavy wooden hoods, or boxes, so as to make such impacts less damaging. The wooden cover over the wheel served another purpose as well, for previously water kicked up by the paddle wheels when in motion had splashed on deck and been a nuisance: with the wheels covered the deck could be used more comfortably as a promenade.

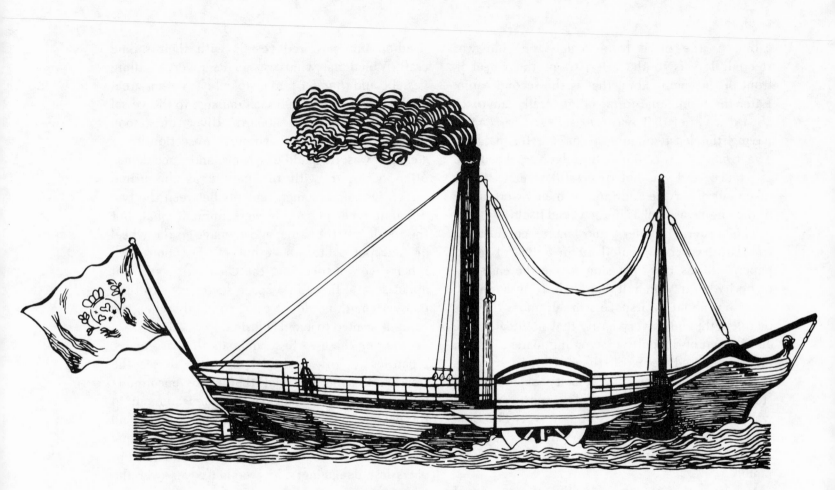

Coastal steamer in Europe, 1816.

Although the *Charlotte* was not a success, Theodore Lawrance did not give up the idea of running a steamboat service. He built a second steamer, the *Hope*, which was launched in 1815. It was 59½ feet long, 10½ feet wide and was put into service on the Severn River plying between Gloucester and Worcester. The *Hope* had an interesting history that illustrates the varied careers of many early steamboats. Lawrance owned the *Hope* until the end of 1815, when he sold it to a Bristol man who nine months later sold it to a lumber company. By then it was "too slow to be agreeable and too crank [apt to capsize] to feel safe." Enlarged and improved, it was still operating in 1822 in Southampton, again as a passenger vessel. Then it was sold to Spanish owners and worked on the Guadalquivir River between Sanlúcar de Barrameda and Seville.

The first steamboat to voyage on the open waters of Europe for any distance was the *Elizabeth*. Built in Scotland in 1813 it went from Glasgow to Liverpool in England and was operated by three young men, none of them older than nineteen. Details of registry and other pertinent facts concerning this steamer are not known, and if it had not been for the reporting of the misadventures of the three young men the vessel would, in all probability, be completely forgotten. With bad weather, a faulty compass, a broken paddle wheel, and engine trouble the steamboat battled its way southward. The *Elizabeth* was carried by the sea's drift from the coast of Wales nearly to the coast of Ireland while the engine was being repaired.

The first steamboat that became famous for making a long voyage on open water in Europe was the *Duke of Argyll*, built at Port Glasgow, Scotland, in 1814 by Alexander Martin. In April 1815 the owners in London asked that it be sent to the Thames River. The voyage was described in one of the first works ever written on steam navigation. Called *Dissertation on Steam Packets,* it was printed in 1818, although it had been written earlier by Captain Dodd who commanded the *Duke of Argyll* on its open water voyage.

Captain Dodd's detailed story of the voyage includes encounters with heavy gales, high winds and waves, and a nearly fatal accident among treacherous rocks. But the most important feature of the tale which sets this early open-water voyage apart from others is that there were passengers aboard the *Duke of Argyll*. It must have been a fairly seaworthy-looking craft to attract paying customers who trusted their lives in the hands of Captain Dodd on this vessel. Despite a warning that it would surely sink if it encountered rough weather, passengers boarded and stayed aboard.

People were so interested in steamboats at that time that when the vessel stopped at Portsmouth, Captain Dodd had to ask the admiral of the port to supply a guard to contain the curious crowds who rushed aboard to examine this new-fangled packet. *The Times* of London announced on July 8, 1815, that the craft is a "rapid, capacious, and splendid vessel, which lately accomplished a voyage of 1,500 miles, has twice crossed St. George's Channel, and came round the Land's End with a rapidity unknown before in naval history. She has the peculiar advantage of proceeding either by sails or steam, separated or united, by which means the public have the pleasing certainty of never being detained on the water after dark, much less one or two nights, which frequently occurred with the old packets." The "old packets" were the sailing packets so popular at the time for coastal and ocean voyages.

The account continues by stating that "her cabins are spacious, and are fitted up with all that elegance could suggest, or all that personal comfort requires, presenting a choice library, backgammon boards, draught tables [for playing checkers], and other means of amusement. For the express purpose of combining delicacy with comfort a female servant tends upon the ladies." This report was written by an editor of *The Times* after he and his family made the trip from London to Margate. As few as ten passengers were aboard on the first trips, but after the glowing story in *The Times* the vessel carried as many as three hundred and fifty passengers aboard for a single run.

The *Duke of Argyll* is an excellent example of the size and power of steamers working in Europe in the second decade of the nineteenth century. It was not a large or powerful vessel, being 78½ feet long, and having a fourteen horse-power engine. (Modern outboard motorboats use engines that range from as little as four horse-power to two hundred and eighty.) The name of the *Duke of Argyll* was changed to the *Thames* when it began service at London.

Russia, Sweden, Prussia, and other European countries were soon following the Scots' example and putting steamboats into service on coastal, lake, and river runs. In 1815 the *Elizabeth* was operating on the Neva River in Russia; in 1816 the *Stockholmshäxan* (*Witch of Stockholm*) was undergoing trials in Sweden; in Prussia the same year the *Prinzessin Charlotte von Preussen* was launched. Also in 1816 the eighty-foot-long *Hibernia* began a successful run between England

and Ireland; service between France and England soon followed introducing the famous cross-Channel steam packets. It was not long afterward that Rotterdam-to-Hull steamboats were introduced.

Europeans, in turn, introduced the steamboat to other areas of the world. As early as 1819 the Nawab of Oudh in India employed an Englishman to build a fifty-foot steamer powered by an engine brought from England. This was probably the first steamboat in the East to be armed: it was fitted with two swivel guns.

A few of the many notices in American newspapers concerning the launching of European steamboats give an idea of the world-wide interest in the new engine-powered vessels. On June 7, 1817: "A steam-boat has arrived at Hamburg from Berlin in 35 hours 25 minutes the distance being 72 leagues. [A league is usually calculated as about three miles.] It is destined to ply between these two cities constantly." August 30, 1817: "A steam boat has been launched at Seville, Spain. The King has decreed that all new invented instruments [steamboats] may be imported free of duty."

France, of course, had many steamers operating on its rivers and open waters by the 1820s. Some of these were built in Scotland, but most were locally built. Jouffroy, the originator of successful steam-powered vessels, obtained a patent for a steamboat design on April 23, 1816, then built and operated the *Charles-Philippe* which worked on the Seine. On September 6, 1817, an American newspaper reported that "a *steam boat,* on a principle that makes explosion impossible, is said to have been invented in France." This safety device was, as Baron de Gerstner wrote in the 1830s, something not seen in America. "Seldom they have here, as they do in Europe, fixed in the boiler a plate of a composition which melts at a certain degree of heat, and the fire becomes extinguished by the water." Still, there were many explosions in Europe. All these early steamboats in Europe were experimental vessels: they were blunt, slow-moving wooden craft. Their designs varied greatly, from the twin-hulled *Prinzessin Charlotte von Preussen* that had three rudders and a paddle wheel working between the double hull, to the *Elizabeth* with its brick chimney on a double-ended barge. The *Stockholmshäxan* was a typical sloop fitted with two masts, the forward mast carrying a square sail and the aftermast gaff rigged. The unusual aspect of this steamboat was that it was driven by a four horse-power engine turning a screw propeller, one of the first propeller experiments in Europe.

Early European river steamer.

Gradually the boilers, the engines, and the paddle wheels were all improved on steamboats in Europe. Robertson Buchanan of Glasgow patented a "feathering" paddle wheel as early as 1813. "Feathering" floats on paddle wheels entered and left the water vertically, and not at an oblique angle as floats had done previously. The result was a greater power and efficiency in the use of the wheel. The bluntness of many early European steamers gave way to more graceful wedge-shaped bows, and slowly wooden hulls gave way to hulls constructed of iron.

The earliest known iron vessel in the West (the Orient had a number of iron-covered vessels used as war ships) was built in 1777, but it was more of a plaything than a working vessel: some reports give the length as twelve feet, other reports mention similar diminutive measurements. Ten years later John Wilkinson, an iron founder in England, was the first to test the belief that "iron won't swim."

Wilkinson was a great promoter of ironwork, and he was extremely fond of publicity: he touted his ironware as if it were truly a rare commodity. His fertile imagination soon conceived the idea of constructing an iron barge. Hundreds of spectators gathered for the launching of the first iron craft certain that it would sink. This barge was

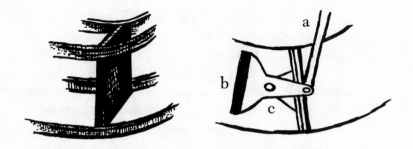

(Left) *Early paddle wheel with rigid bucket.* (Right) *Feathering paddle wheel. The term "feathering" was adopted from the sport of rowing, where it meant to turn the oar so that it leaves the water and cuts the air edgewise. As the wheel turns, the rod (a) adjusts the bucket (b) that is flexibly hinged to the wheel (c). In this manner the bucket enters and leaves the water at approximately a right angle, producing maximum purchase, or seizing force.*

named the *Trial*. Actually it was not an iron vessel at all, but like the earlier Oriental craft merely covered with iron plate—its stern and stem posts were also wooden. As the *Trial* splashed great geysers of water at its launching the crowd laughed and applauded, waiting for it to sink. To the amazement of many the iron barge floated, and although it was successful, iron plate was not commonly used on ships until sixty years later. Many people plainly thought it unnatural that metal could float on water. Of course this is true: metal itself does not float unless built into the form of a hull. A ship—or any container—sinks into the water until it has displaced a volume of water equal to its own weight. If the upper edges are still above water then, it floats. Even though iron ships did not sink, most people believed they would soon rust and spring leaks.

Gradually the resistance to metal vessels diminished. In 1818 the iron barge *Vulcan* was built near Glasgow, and this vessel is supposed to have been in service as a coal barge as late as 1875. Next came the *Aaron Manby* built in 1821. This was the first iron steamboat built. It was constructed for Sir Charles Napier and Aaron Manby at the Horsley Iron Works near Birmingham. Sent to London in sections and assembled, it then underwent trials in May of 1822. The London *Courier* of May 15, 1822, called it "the most complete specimen of workmanship in the iron way that has even been witnessed." The *Aaron Manby* was originally built for work in shoal waters, but it was bought by a Paris firm and put into passenger service on the Seine. The first iron steamboat in America was built by John Elgar of York, Pennsylvania, in 1825. It was constructed on a tributary of the Susquehanna River called Codorus Creek and was named the *Codorus*.

The York (Pennsylvania) *Gazette* of November 8, 1825, gives the following account of the *Codorus:* "The boat has sixty feet keel, nine feet beam, and is three feet high. It is composed entirely of sheet iron, riveted with iron rivets, and the ribs, which are one foot apart, are strips of sheet iron, which by their peculiar form are supposed to possess thrice the strength of the same weight of iron in the square platform. The whole weight of iron in the boat, when she shall be finished, will be fourteen hundred pounds. That of the wood work, deck, cabin, etc., will be two thousand six hundred pounds, being together two tons. The steam engine, the boiler included, will weigh two tons, making the whole weight of the boat and engine but four tons. She will draw, when launched, but five inches and every additional ton which may be put on board of her will sink her one inch in the water.

"The engine is upon the high pressure principle, calculated to bear six hundred pounds to the inch, and the engine will be worked with not more than one hundred pounds to the inch. It will have an eight horse power engine and the boiler is formed so that the anthracite coal will be exclusively used to produce steam. The ingenuity with which the boiler is constructed, and its entire competency for burning the Susquehanna coal are entitled to particular notice, and the inventors, if they succeed in this experiment will be entitled to the thanks of every Pennsylvanian." They did not succeed and wood was used as fuel.

Sheet iron from the Codorus, *the first metal steamer in the United States, based on a sketch from Lewis Miller's* Chronicles of York *(Pennsylvania) 1789–1870.*

CHAPTER 9

Traveling on Steamboats

THE STEAMBOAT caused great changes in the lives of Americans. The interchange of goods and people between the settled Atlantic seaboard and the growing western portions of the country increased at an astounding rate. Traders and travelers who previously had spent much money and a good deal of time going by coach, sail, barge, or wagon benefited enormously when steamboats came into use.

An idea of what river travel was like before the appearance of the steamboat can be gained from an advertisement in a 1794 newspaper. The *Centinel of the Northwestern Territory* ran this notice for a packet boat company operating between Pittsburgh and Cincinnati: "A separate cabin from that designed for the men is partitioned off in each boat, for accommodating ladies on their passage. Conveniences [toilets] are constructed on board each boat, so as to render landing unnecessary, as it might, at times, be attended with danger. [Attack by Indians.] . . .Passengers will be supplied with provisions and liquors of all kinds of the first quality, at the most reasonable rates possible."

The accommodations and regulations used on these river packets were the same for early steamers. Rules and regulations were posted as has been seen in a previous chapter. Also, the physical makeup of steamboats followed packet and barge design at first. Passengers slept in curtained bunks divided by a narrow aisle. There was a dining room aboard (usually the men's cabin, but sometimes a separate section was set aside for dining), and a bar. "The bar and gentleman's cabin," as James Stuart, a visitor from Scotland, wrote concerning New York harbor steamers, "contained a great variety of eatables and drinkables such as Bologna sausages, hung-beef, biscuits, and all sorts of confectionary; with wines, spirits, oranges, lemons, limes."

In Europe on the early steamers first-class travel was a delightful way to cover short distances: seldom did passage in Europe last a full day. The crossing of the Channel from the Continent to England was thought a fairly arduous voyage—it was slightly more than twenty miles—and even at four to eight miles per hour on the earliest steamers this trip did not take long to complete. Coastal and river voyages of a day or little more were common, but compared to the distances covered by steamboats on the rivers of the American West, these European voyages seem mere excursions. Even on the earliest of American steamers, travels of one or two thousand miles were everyday affairs, and such voyages lasted for weeks.

Steerage passengers in Europe were often described as sullen, dirty, and drunk, but in the first-class cabin, manners and decorum reigned. Such decorum was not maintained on American steam vessels for a number of reasons. There were no "classes" on American boats: everyone traveled in equal comfort or distress, depending on the conditions of the vessel. A form of steerage passage did appear on steamboats with the separation of the decks, when travel on the main deck with the cargo was cheaper and rougher by far than travel

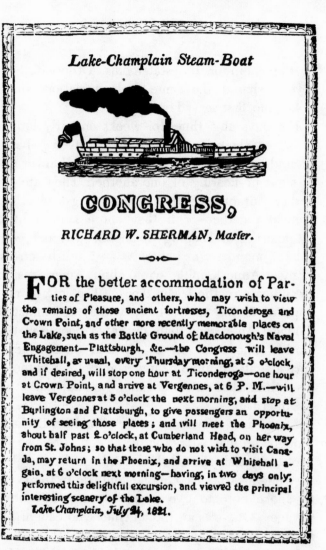

Lake-Champlain Steam-Boat

CONGRESS,

RICHARD W. SHERMAN, Master.

—◦|◦—

FOR the better accommodation of Parties of Pleasure, and others, who may wish to view the remains of those ancient fortresses, Ticonderoga and Crown Point, and other more recently memorable places on the Lake, such as the Battle Ground of Macdonough's Naval Engagement—Plattsburgh, &c.—the Congress will leave Whitehall, as usual, every Thursday morning, at 5 o'clock, and if desired, will stop one hour at Ticonderoga—one hour at Crown Point, and arrive at Vergennes, at 6 P. M.—will leave Vergennes at 5 o'clock the next morning, and stop at Burlington and Plattsburgh, to give passengers an opportunity of seeing those places ; and will meet the Phoenix, about half past 2 o'clock, at Cumberland Head, on her way from St. Johns; so that those who do not wish to visit Canada, may return in the Phoenix, and arrive at Whitehall again, at 6 o'clock next morning—having, in two days only, performed this delightful excursion, and viewed the principal interesting scenery of the Lake.

Lake-Champlain, July 24, 1821.

An announcement of a pleasure cruise by steamer in the early 1800s.

in the cabin or the staterooms. Otherwise, everyone shared the same accommodations on a first-come, first-served basis.

For days at a time, for weeks on early longer voyages, these passengers with diverse backgrounds spent their time together, hardly ever out of sight or hearing of one another. They ate together, drank together, sang songs together, danced together—or if they chose kept a little bit apart. But keeping to oneself was not considered mannerly or polite. As an English actress, Frances Anne Kemble, wrote about Americans on steamboats in the early 1800s: "The gift of gab appears to me to be more widely diseminated amongst Americans than any other people in the world." She went on to say that on steamers: "privacy at any time or under any circumstances, 'tis a thing that enters not into the imagination of an American."

Americans traveling with Charles Dickens thought he was "stand-offish" or rude because he kept to himself aboard the steamboats he traveled on while in America. On one long trip in the West he spoke only to two people during the entire voyage. (One was an Indian chief who caught his fancy.) His fellow travelers thought there was something decidedly wrong with Mr. Dickens. He, for his part, thought there was something quite seriously out of joint with Americans. He disapproved of the way people came up to him and shook his hand, or patted him on the back and began talking without the slightest formality.

The behavior Europeans saw on American steamers shocked them and often created a very poor impression of life in America. Usually, such tourists had enough money to travel first class when at home in Europe: often they resented being classed with the "mob," and sometimes they were plainly frightened out of their wits when unceremoniously thrown together with the poorer segment of society. But Dickens and other Europeans were not alone in this dislike for the openness (some called it "pushiness") in the American character. A Philadelphian, Samuel Breck, had this to say: "The rich and the poor, the educated and the ignorant, the polite and the vulgar, all herd together in this modern improvement in travelling. The consequence is a complete amalgamation. Master and servant sleep heads and points on the cabin floor of the steamer, feed at the same table, sit in each other's laps, as it were. . . Talk of ladies on a steamboat. . . There are none."

If this is how some Americans felt, it is easy to understand the dismay of Europeans with a strong sentiment against any means of travel that brought the wealthy and the poor, or the noble and the peasant, to a common level. As Frances Trollope, mother of the famous English novelist, put it when she wrote about her stay in America (she ran a dry goods store in Cincinnati for a short time in 1827): "The gentlemen in the cabin (we had no ladies) would certainly, neither from their language, manners, nor appearance, have received that designation in Europe." About travel on a western steamboat: "The total want of all the usual courtesies of the table, the voracious rapidity with which the viands were seized and devoured, the strange uncouth phrases and pronunciations; . . . the frightful manner of feeding with their knives, till the whole blade seemed to enter into the mouth; and the still more frightful manner of cleaning the teeth afterwards with a pocket knife, soon forced us to feel that we were not surrounded by the generals, colonels, and majors of the old world; and that the dinner hour was to be anything rather than an hour of enjoyment." The scenes described so vividly by Mrs. Trollope would not have been encountered by a "cabin" passenger on a European steamboat—although they could easily have been witnessed in any of the rowdy beef-houses that served as restaurants in London.

If travel by steamboat was so disagreeable in the early days, why did such tourists use the steamboat at all? A Frenchman traveling from New York to New Orleans in 1816–17 gave the answer: "I must repeat again and again that the American stagecoaches are untrustworthy. . . It is impossible to conceive the frightful inconvenience of these vehicles." He goes on to say that you get soaked, crushed, shaken, thrown about and bumped every foot of the way: coaches are shattered, horses killed, passengers crippled by the many stagecoach accidents. He ends by telling the reader that: "To pass from the steamboat to the stage, especially in bad weather, is to descend from paradise to hell."

Criticism came not only from Europeans. Intelligent and reasonable Americans also had difficulty in hiding a disdain for their fellow passengers on southern and western steamboats. Frederick Olmsted wrote that the businessmen, cotton-planters, and emigrants on the steamboat *Fashion* out of Mobile, were: "usually well dressed, but were a rough, coarse style of people, drinking a great deal, and most of the time under a little alcoholic excitement. Not sociable, except with the topics of cotton, land, and negroes, were started; interested, however, in talk about theatres and the turf; very profane; often showing the handles of concealed weapons about their persons, but not quarrelsome, avoiding disputes and altercations, and respectful to one another in forms of words; very ill-informed, except on plantation business: their language ungrammatical, idiomatic, and extravagant . . . I found that, more than any people I had ever seen, they were unrateable by dress, taste, forms, and expenditures."

Olmsted goes on to say that they had self-possession, confidence, coarseness, low tastes, frankness, reserve, recklessness, self-restraint, extravagance, and penuriousness. In other words his traveling companions were "ordinary" people. This account of travel on steamboats in America simply shows the diversity in human natures and how one passenger analyzed his fellow travelers. It adds to the picture of steamboat travel, but as Walt Whitman said: "You shall listen to all sides and filter them for yourself."

Accidents on steamboats from explosion of boilers, fire, and other reasons were not at all extraordinary on the early steamers, and later. The history of one explosion is given in 1842: "The *Oliver Evans*, seventy-five tons, was built at Pittsburgh, by George Evans; engine his patent. Left Pittsburgh, December 1816, for New Orleans. Burst one of her boilers in April 1817, at Point Coupee, by which eleven men, chiefly passengers, were killed. Never did much business afterwards." There were over fifty steamer explosions in the United States before the year 1831. Many people were killed (approximately three hundred) and wounded (over a hundred), and although accidents occurred in greater number on sailing vessels because there were more of them, fear of such accidents on steamers kept some travelers from using them.

William C. Redfield of Connecticut devised a safety barge for the use of those who were afraid to travel on steam vessels: these craft were simply attractive barges towed by steamboats. Redfield's company put out an announcement that: "Passengers on board the safety barges will not be in the least exposed to any accident by reason of the fire or steam on board the steamboats."

These barges were popular during the latter part of the 1820s; according to Thomas L. McKenney, a commissioner of the Interior Department, a journey on one was extremely pleasant. He sailed on one of the first ever built in 1826 and wrote: "I was struck with the admirable invention." They were four decks high: the men slept on the main deck where there was a bar; on the next deck up the women slept, and forward was a room where the men dressed, shaved and read; the deck above this was an indoor promenade and lounge; the grand promenade was on the top deck, with awning protection from sun and rain.

Part of the interest in Mr. McKenney's record of his trip comes from the fact that he makes particu-

A safety barge towed by a steamboat. These barges were popular during the latter part of the 1820s. They were often four decks high: On the main deck were a bar and sleeping quarters for men, and on the next deck up the women slept. Above this was an indoor promenade and lounge, and the grand promenade was the highest, open deck.

lar mention of staterooms. It is often thought that staterooms on steamboats did not come into use until 1836 on the Mississippi. The story goes that an inventive captain, Isaiah Seller, built rooms such as those used in hotels aboard his steamboat the *Prairie* and named them after individual States of the Union. But there was one more State than there were rooms, so he called the house on the hurricane deck the "Texas." Actually, the word stateroom goes back many centuries to the 1600s, when in a nautical sense it was used to designate a captain's or superior officer's room on board a ship. On steamboats the word stateroom was applied to a cabin, usually richly decorated.

Although no accidents occurred on safety barges, there was one serious drawback for many people—they were slow. After the novelty for such craft wore off passengers once again flocked back to the steamboats, and the safety barges were converted to freight barges.

The pilot house on steamers did not come into wide use until the 1830s and then only took hold slowly and often in quite astonishing form; some looked like fancy, domed hothouses, and others like miniature churches. Only later did they become the simple, no-nonsense affairs commonly seen today. Two reasons for their late appearance were that most steamboats did not have an upper deck until the late 1820s, and that steamboats were at first steered with a tiller at the stern. A pilot stood at the bow and the course was called out and relayed to the helmsman who steered by using a pole attached to the rudder. Signals to the engine room were given either by calling them down or thumping the deck. It seems odd, perhaps, to think of steamboats without the pilot at the wheel faithfully guiding the vessel on river or bay. But in those days the steering wheel, first introduced as a navigational aid in the 1700s, was not especially popular on American coastal craft either.

By the 1820s American steamboats were making trips between Louisville and New Orleans in about a week. Many passenger boats were becoming more complex and elegant in construction. Fulton is reported as having made his second steamboat "into a floating palace, gay with ornamental paintings, gilding and polished woods," thereby setting the tone for all later steamers. That they were all comfortable and pleasantly decorated from the beginning is sometimes thought to be the case, but this is not true.

The steamer *Eagle,* built in 1813, was fairly typical of early steam vessels. Most of the freight room was filled with wood and the ladies' cabin in the rear had very small, narrow berths. Between this cabin and the engine was the small, dark dining room where the berths used by the men were situated.

Even as late as 1837 bunk-bed arrangements were still common. Captain F. Marryat writing in *A Diary in America* recalled that when he embarked at midnight in an Albany steamer fitted out as a night boat he went to the cabin and found: "two rows of bed-places on each side of the immense cabin, running fore and aft, three other rows in the center, each of these five rows having three bed-places, one over the other. There were upward of 500 people, lying in every variety of posture." He said the air in this huge cabin was so oppressive that he went on deck rather than stay below.

Other descriptions of the Albany night boats in the early days of steamboating clearly show how different the reports of different travelers could be. Thomas S. Woodcock in his *New York to Niagara Journal* of 1836 wrote: "Left New York in the Steam Boat Albany. . . fare is $3. Meals extra. The night line leaves at 5 o'clock and is fitted up with elegant Berths for sleeping and is certainly the most convenient way of traveling . . ."

Another traveler, James Hall, in 1842 reported on Mississippi steamers, saying that: "Large and cheerful parties. . . meet on board the steamboats, and, as they must necessarily be several days together, they endeavor to accommodate themselves to each other, and to pass the time agreeably. . . Music and dancing are the chief amusements; and at night, when the spacious cabin of one of our leviathan boats is lighted up, enlivened by the merry notes of the violin, and filled with well dressed persons, it seems more like a floating palace than a mere conveyance for wayfarers."

But John James Audubon, writing to Hall the year after the glowing description above appeared in print, had this to say about a trip he made on the Mississippi: "And such a steamer as we have come in from Louisville here! The very filthiest of all filthy old rat-traps I ever travelled in; and the fare worse, certainly much worse, and so scanty withal that our worthy commander could not have given us another meal had we been detained a night longer."

There was a feature about all these boats that at first disturbed many travelers, and Charles Dickens gives a very sharp picture of it: "Directly you have left the wharf, all the life, and stir, and bustle of the packet ceases. You wonder for a long time how she goes on, for there seems nobody in charge of her; and when another of these dull machines comes splashing by, you feel quite indignant with it, as a sullen, cumbrous, ungraceful,

A steam brig for coastal travel in the early 1820s.

unshiplike leviathan; quite forgetting that the vessel you are aboard of is its very counterpart."

Dickens's description reflects the feeling that there was something "unshiplike" about steamers. On sailing vessels the rigging sings, the sails boom and slap, the deck creaks—the ship seems alive—and all depends on the captain and the crew at all times. The crew is visible, working in all weather. The captain can be heard giving orders. The passenger is involved in a human endeavor that interests him keenly. A voyage on a sailing vessel may be frightening, difficult, and physically trying, even at times boring, but the passenger is almost

*An early costal steamer, the type Charles Dickens
thought so "unshiplike."*

always involved, no matter how passively, in the fight against wind and weather.

This did not seem to be true on most steamboat trips. The engine beats, the steam hisses eerily, the vessel may quiver a bit, but often the passengers do not feel "at sea," nor "on the water." The crew is mostly out of sight below and the pilot in the pilot house above. The captain often behaves more like a host than a seaman. It seemed to many early travelers that anyone could operate an "unshiplike" steamboat. It was only in the late periods of

steamboat travel that steamboats were filled with the "distinctive aroma of soap, clean linens, steam and saltwater," and in movement one felt "the unforgettable surging motion as the paddle wheels thrust into the water," as Robert H. Burgess wrote in the Baltimore *Sun* of February 27, 1972.

The slowness and undependability of early steamers is another feature often forgotten. It was not unusual for passengers to miss a steamboat at the landing, yet have little difficulty in catching up with it by following on foot. Or, to board a steamboat scheduled to leave at ten on Tuesday, and then have to wait two or three days for various repairs to be made before leaving the wharf. Delays of two and three days also took place while the captain waited for enough passengers to board to make the trip a paying proposition. The boats were poorly constructed and lasted only a few seasons—frequently enough, only a few months: by and large American steamboats were rickety, short-lived craft, only the larger vessels were built to last.

The spirit of restlessness which gripped Americans in the first half of the 1800s, however, and the insistence on speed over comfort, soon produced steamboats that were navigating at speeds far surpassing any European steamer. This quest for speed introduced an exciting pastime into the steamboat scene: racing. Steamboat racing became common in all regions of the United States.

In the first decade of the nineteenth century John Stevens was so proud of the swiftness of his steamers (8 to 10 m.p.h.) that he could not resist racing a Livingston-Fulton boat (4 to 8 m.p.h.). As an observer wrote: "When two steamboats happen to get alongside each other, the passengers will encourage the captains to run a race . . ."

Casualties and boiler explosions were common during such races. This did not, however, deter steamboat captains. A report of one of the greatest races of the 1830s is given in an 1838 newspaper; the two steamers mentioned ran from Stonington, Connecticut, to New York City. It read: "For ten or a dozen miles down [Long Island] Sound there was no perceptible change in the relative position of the boats. Then dense clouds of smoke poured from *Lexington,* a sheet of flame shot up from her stack, her wheels turned swifter, and a cheer burst from passengers as they realized the gap between them and *Richmond* was closing. It was an anxious moment on board *Richmond* for *Lexington* was gaining fast. Where was Captain Townsend? There was no reply. He was not to be found. But the movements on board *Lexington* had not escaped his eye. The moment that the boat left Stonington men had been set picking out the most

resinous wood and piling it for immediate use. The engineer had been tightening bolts and screws, and *Richmond* was ready for the race.

"At the first puffs of black smoke from *Lexington,* Captain Townsend had rushed to the engine room and was consulting the engineer. 'Oh, she can stand considerably more,' said that functionary: and the Captain answered, 'Well, put in the fat wood and let her go.' She did go. Volumes of smoke poured from her funnel, and the roar of her fires could be heard all over the boat. A column of flame stood a pillar of fire above her. She trembled at every revolution of her wheels. The water seethed and boiled beneath her, fire and smoke were round about her overhead. She advanced like the rush of an avalanche—she was a moving volcano. Slowly, steadily, she moved away from *Lexington;* wider and wider grew the interval between them, until at last *Richmond* dashed between the rocks at Hell Gate and *Lexington* was seen no more until she came by an hour after *Richmond* had made fast to her pier."

Racing was one way of making a voyage interesting. There were other, less risky, pastimes. Drinking and gambling were permitted on all boats. A few passengers were fleeced by professional gamblers who sometimes worked in teams, but on many steamboats (as well as in saloons) a limit was posted on the amount of money allowed to be lost during a game. For example, a wall plaque might remind passengers: "Card games limited to $12.50."

Most steamers were of small or medium size: the scows thirty feet upward; the freight boats with only moderately comfortable passenger accommodations ranging from fifty to eighty feet long and in the early days from 31 tons to 300 tons. Later the tonnage rose on these moderate-size boats to average out at about 400 tons but ranging from 200 to 900 tons. The steamers most often associated with steamboating in those days were the large passenger vessels used by people rich enough to voyage in style. In the East these were the Hudson boats about which Captain F. Marryat wrote in 1837: "When I first saw one of the largest [boats] sweep around the battery, with two decks, the upper one screened with snow-white awnings—the gay dresses of the ladies—the variety of colors—it reminded me of a floating garden. . . ."

On the Hudson River steamer the *Francis Skiddy*, William Makepeace Thackeray, the English author, traveled during his lecture tour in 1852. This vessel had a speed of about 25 m.p.h. made possible by the use of four iron boilers situated on the guards. It was launched in 1852, the year Thackeray traveled on it, and was con-sidered the handsomest steamer on the Hudson at the time. Thackeray wrote: "The queerest [sight] was one of the Albany Steamers—called the *Francis Skiddy*. Fancy Vauxhall [a fashionable public garden at Lambeth, London] glorified fresh gilt decorated, carpeted and afloat and theres this wonderful ark. It's an immense moving saloon 200 feet long with little state-rooms in each side furnished some of them in such a way that the Duchess of Sutherland herself never had any thing so grand to sleep in—white brocade silk curtains and gold bullion hangings and velvet carpets and porcelain ye Gods such porcelain!"

In the West the *Memphis, Sultana,* and other well-known steamboats were written and sung about. But this opulent era passed, and steamboats in America developed into the sturdy, practical vessels that many remember.

Passenger service in the East continued to be substantial into the 1900s, but in the West passenger steamboats went into decline after 1860. T. W. Knox writing in 1886 noted that this decline came about: "owing to the extension of railways in every direction, and their reduction of the time required for a long journey. Ordinarily the best of the steamboats require five or six days for the trip from New Orleans to St. Louis or Louisville, which the railway can easily make in three."

CHAPTER 10

The Challenge of the Oceans

EXPERIENCE with the early and rather primitive steamships showed that steam vessels needed to be enormously improved before long ocean voyages could be successfully accomplished. To a few of the more energetic and farsighted ship owners and builders this challenge generated a drive to prove that steamers could conquer the tempestuous Atlantic. The vessels such men produced at first were isolated novelties, and successful steam navigation on the ocean did not become important or gain significance until steam was already in general use on many rivers and bays throughout the world. The rivers of America and the waters of the Firth of Clyde had been the battlegrounds on which steam-powered vessels fought for, and won, acceptance.

The Atlantic ocean, the first ocean crossed by steamers, is a formidable body of water covering nearly twenty-five percent of the earth's surface.

The crossing between New York and European ports covers over three thousand miles of open sea with dangers from violent storms, icebergs, and towering waves. Along the coast there are such hazards to navigation as the storms off Cape Hatteras, where many steamers and sailing vessels have been wrecked. Besides the physical threats encountered by the early steamships, there was another powerful opponent: sailing packets. Sailing packets were fast and comfortable, and from 1818 they were operated as "liners."

A liner is a ship sailing on a strict schedule. The earliest packets used as liners on the ocean were four vessels operating out of New York, the *Amity, Courier, Pacific*, and *James Monroe*. The company operating these vessels was named the "Black Ball Line," and a huge black ball was painted on one of the ships' sails for identification purposes. (At sea a passing vessel could bring back news of the vessel's progress, and when it arrived far outside the port it could be spied through a glass and the information signaled to the main office where preparations for receiving it were immediately gotten underway.)

The Black Ball Line began liner operation in January 1818, although the notice of the company's intention was published as early as October 27, 1817. The New York *Evening Post* ran an advertisement on that day that stated: "In order to furnish frequent and regular conveyances for goods and passengers, the subscribers have undertaken to establish a line of vessels between New York and Liverpool, to sail from each place on a certain day of every month throughout the year." These ships would sail "full or not full," while unscheduled ships waited to receive all the cargo they could obtain and as complete a passenger list as possible.

The idea of a scheduled run did not originate with these packets; mail brigs operating between Falmouth and New York had been running on schedule since 1756, and steamboats from their inception had scheduled runs. Shorter packet runs on the Hudson and in many other places were also run on schedules for many years before the ocean liners came into existence. Still, it was a new idea on the Atlantic passenger run, and it proved

enormously successful, especially since the packets were fast—out of New York 18–20 days across, and back in 22–25 days on some of the faster runs. Their accommodations were particularly appealing to the traveler of the day. Traveling on a sailing packet Herman Melville wrote: "Went on deck again, & remained till near midnight. The scene was indescribable. I never saw such sailing before."

Despite their sailing abilities and the pleasures found aboard for the privileged passengers (steerage was sometimes a brutal experience), the packet was eventually replaced by steamships on the ocean. The earliest steamers went to sea simply to get from one port to another as the *Maid of Orleans* did in 1819 when it steamed from Philadelphia to New Orleans, then up the Mississippi to St. Louis. But such voyages were of no importance in carrying forward the development of oceanic steamers. In Europe, both England and Scotland sent vessels long distances along the coast and across the Irish Sea: these events played only a minor role in voyages on the open sea.

There were few oceanographic adventures of any significance during the second and third decades of the nineteenth century, but there were a number of attempts to use steam that had meaning in maritime circles. In 1819 *The Times* of

London printed an article that appeared on Tuesday, May 11, stating: "A new steam vessel called the *Savannah* packet of 300 tons burden has been built in New York for the express purpose of carrying passengers across the Atlantic. She is to come to Liverpool direct. A trial has been made with her from New York to Savannah. . ."

The *Savannah* was a sailing packet with auxiliary steam-power: it was not half sail, half steam but a sailing vessel equipped with paddle wheels (collapsible) and an engine. It was built in New York City in 1818 and measured 98 feet 6 inches between perpendiculars, and 109 feet from figurehead (the partial figure of a man) to taffrail. The voyage across the Atlantic is only known from newspaper reports and scant entries in the *Savannah's* log book. The captain was Moses Rogers, the same man who had operated Stevens's *Phoenix* in its run from New York to Delaware Bay ten years earlier. The vessel carried neither passengers nor cargo; it was difficult even to get a crew to undertake the voyage because the idea of using steam at sea seemed so risky.

It is unfortunate that no one wrote a well-researched book about the *Savannah* at the time of its crossing, for hardly any of the accounts made at the time agree on such an essential point as the number of hours the engine was in use. For that

Figurehead carvings often represented the person for whom the ship was named.

matter hardly any two accounts, even today, agree on such matters concerning the *Savannah*. Both coal and wood were used as fuel, and concerning the amount of fuel used there is also some disagreement as well as guesswork done by a number of people. The important point, however, is not the amount used but the fact that ocean-going steam vessels were fueled with coal. Coal (fossilized vegetable matter that has become carbonized) is a more efficient fuel than firewood: a ton of coal gives off much more heat energy than a ton of wood. By using coal the range of the steam vessel was greatly extended. This simple fact was the basic reason for the success of the steam vessel at sea.

The voyage across the Atlantic is supposed to have taken a little over 29 days, and the time under steam ranged from 85 to 100 hours. These statistics are of some interest, but the main feature concerning the *Savannah* in the development of oceanic steam vessels was summarized by Captain Rogers, who said to Christopher Hughes, the American ambassador in Sweden, where the *Savannah* touched after leaving England: "I know sir, that I am spending and losing money in the expedition: but I have satisfied the world that the thing is practicable."

Many oceanic steam-powered vessels were built along the eastern coast of the United States during this period. The *Albermarle,* built at Baltimore in 1818–19, made voyages between Baltimore—New York and Baltimore—North Carolina. A number of such vessels were employed along the coast. One of the most interesting, because it was a success, was the *Robert Fulton.* It was built at New York by Henry Eckford for David Dunham & Company and put into the New York, Havana, New Orleans passenger and freight service in 1820. The engine was used only for auxiliary power, but it was used much more often than *Savannah's* engine.

The maiden voyage to New Orleans began on April 25, 1820, covered over two thousand miles, and took eighteen days. On the voyage back, the actual steaming time from Havana to Charleston was over fifty hours. There were about seventy first-class passengers on the initial northbound voyage, and it served many hundreds of passengers during the five years it remained in service. The vessels that plied the coasts of America and Europe in the 1820s and early '30s were the forerunners of oceanic steam vessels: a cross-Channel packet was, in fact, the first transatlantic steamer.

In December 1824 a French steam-auxiliary sailing vessel, *La Caroline* (originally *Galibi*), sailed between Brest and Cayenne in French Guiana, South America. In 1825 the 120 horse-power engine on the English ship *Enterprise* was used now and again on a voyage between London and Calcutta, India. In 1825 another steamer was working on the coast off Ecuador. Called the *Telica,* or *Telca,* it was owned and commanded by a Mr. Mitrovich. It had crossed from Europe under sail and was fitted out with machinery at Guayaquil. Delays under steam and constant complaints by the passengers annoyed Mr. Mitrovich who discharged a pistol in a barrel of gunpowder and blew up the ship, passengers, crew, and himself.

The *Curaçao* made several trips across the ocean in 1827, from the Netherlands to the Netherland Antilles. The *Curaçao's* first crossing took twenty-eight days, and steam was often used. It returned to the Netherlands and the next year made the crossing again when steam was used continuously for the first thirteen days. This was an improvement on earlier sailing vessels using auxiliary steam.

The list of early sailing ships equipped with steam engines is extensive, including the *Rising Star* and the *Royal William,* the latter often supposed to have made the first oceanic crossing solely under steam in 1833. But, although the engines were more efficient than those previously employed on sea voyages, the *Royal William,* according to its captain, often used sail alone.

It was not until the late 1830s that steamships finally succeeded in making the difficult Atlantic crossing. In 1838 it was accomplished by two steam vessels, the *Sirius* and the *Great Western,* and these voyages were made almost completely under steam. (They were steamships equipped with auxiliary sail: sail was used for many years after this on steamers. On one vessel, sail, paddle wheels, and a propeller were used.) The success of these two steamers, especially the financial success of the *Great Western,* went a long way in establishing the superiority of steam over sail in many shipbuilders' and shipowners' minds.

There was a buzz of excitement on both sides of the North Atlantic: the race was on to see which steamship company would be the first to sail a steam vessel between Europe and America. An American, Junius Smith, planned a steamship company with four steamers, two built in Europe and two in the United States. After the *British Queen* (245 feet long and 40 feet wide) and the *President* were built, Smith ran into trouble. The ships were constructed with feathering paddle wheels without the consent of the patent holder for this type of wheel. The ships had to be hurriedly altered, losing a good deal of time for Smith and his associates.

Meanwhile, the competing vessel the *Great Western* was built in Bristol under the direction of Ismabard Brunel. This vessel was designed for ocean voyages and intended to carry well over a hundred passengers. It was smaller than the *British Queen* that Smith was struggling to complete, being 212 feet long and 35 feet wide. But its small size did not hinder its coal-carrying capacity, normally 680 tons, but supposedly able to take on

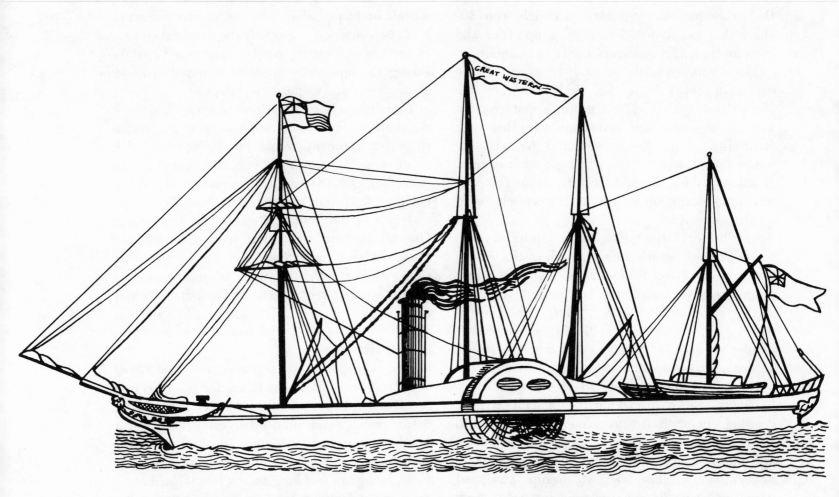

The Great Western, *launched in 1837. The success of this vessel, the first truly oceanic steamer built, went a long way toward establishing the superiority of steam over sail on the oceans of the world.*

as much as 800 tons. The coal was enough for a difficult, slow passage. The transatlantic trip usually took between two and three weeks on these early steamers, and this compared favorably with sailing packet crossings.

The *Great Western* was launched in 1837 when it was towed from Bristol to the Thames River to be fitted out with engines. Completed early in 1838, it underwent trials in March of that year averaging twelve knots under good conditions. At sea this speed fell to nine knots or less, which was about average for steamers in the late 1830s and '40s.

Smith, knowing Brunel's vessel was about to sail, charted a cross-Channel steamer, the *Sirius*, and set out to sea in it in place of the *British Queen* which would not be ready for another three months. The *Sirius* was a good-sized vessel—only 34 feet shorter than the *Great Western*—and its engine was of an advanced design.

The *Sirius* sailed on April 4, 1838, with forty excited passengers, well aware that the *Great Western* would soon follow and perhaps win the race. The weather was fair, and the *Sirius* moved forward at a steady pace. The *Great Western* sailed four days later on the 8th of April with only seven passengers aboard. On the voyage from the Thames back to Bristol there was a fire in the boiler room, and some crew members, as well as many of the passengers, decided not to risk crossing the Atlantic in a ship that might prove unsafe.

On April 23 the *Sirius* arrived in New York and was met by wildly cheering crowds on shore and a bay crowded with boats filled with shouting, waving sightseers. Excitement in the city mounted when it was reported that the *Great Western* was not far out at sea and would also soon arrive. Before its arrival the New York *Herald* put out a special issue, stating: "Arrival of the Sirius Steamer in Seventeen Days from Cork [the actual time was eighteen days, twelve hours], The Beginning of the New Age in Steam Power—the Broad Atlantic Bridged at Last—Annihilation of Space and Time. This morning the city was thrown into a state of glorious excitement at the announcement of the *Sirius* steamer, Capt. Roberts, in 17 days from Cork, Ireland. . . She is now up and anchored off the Battery, where thousands were down gazing at her, early in the morning."

A little over three hours after the *Sirius*'s arrival the *Great Western* reached port and New York celebrated with bands blaring. Parties were given for the captains and their crews, speeches made, toasts drunk, and parades given in honor of the vessels. The *Great Western* had reached New York

The Sirius. Used originally for cross-channel service, it was hired by an American, Junius Smith, and became the first steam vessel to cross the Atlantic almost wholly under steam (1838).

in a little more than fifteen days from Bristol. Both vessels made other round-trip voyages that same year; at last steam-powered vessels had conquered the ocean.

It was not long before regular "lines" of steamers were crossing the Atlantic. The Collins Line, organized in 1848 by E. K. Collins, was one of the first in the United States. Its steamers had such luxury features as steam-heating throughout, a smoke room, a bathroom (an extraordinary feature on land as well as at sea at that time), a barber shop, and many other comforts. The Collins steamers were also well known for the efficiency of their paddle wheels. This line ran from 1850 to 1858 with such widely acclaimed "modern" vessels as the *Pacific, Baltic, Arctic,* and *Atlantic.*

The *Pacific* traveled 330 miles in one day during a voyage in its second year in service, a record that held for speed until 1864. The Collins Line was not a success, for it was run with high cost and plagued by bad luck. The *Arctic* was rammed in a thick fog in 1854; it sank with the loss of eighty-seven lives. The *Pacific* left England one January day in 1856 with forty-five passengers and a crew of a hundred and forty-one: it was never seen again.

There were also many European lines in operation on the ocean shortly after the *Sirius* and *Great Western* made the first successful runs. One of the most important was the Cunard Line whose vessels were built in Scotland under the direction of Robert Napier. This line had a distinct advantage over the other early oceanic steam companies, for it was awarded the mail subsidy by the English government that allowed it to operate at a profit. By 1862 its vessels were the largest and most powerful on the ocean, making the Atlantic crossing in as little as eight days.

These were the early "queens" of the ocean, and travel aboard them was usually very comfortable except for the steerage passengers. This was not the case in other instances, especially in the smaller vessels using steam that went into oceanic operation. James McQueen, writing in 1838, said: "Imagine a small, ill-contrived boat, an old 10-gun brig, as the *Carron* is, for example, of 100-h.p., and 30 to 40 tons of coal on her deck; with a cabin 13′ x 10′, and an after cabin still smaller, both without any means of ventilation, except what two ill-planned, narrow and miserable hatches, when opened, afford. Imagine a vessel like this starting from Jamaica with 10 to 15 passengers, and a crew of 37, still more miserably provided with room and quarters. . . having the boiler immediately adjoining the cabin and sleeping berths, and without any place to stow the luggage belonging to the passengers—and with numerous mail bags crammed into the small sleeping berths, or under the table—and the public will have a faint idea of a government steamboat; wherein under a tropical sun and a tropical rain, the passengers and crew are, with the hatches closed, reduced to the choice, while choked with coal-dust, of being boiled or suffocated." McQueen was describing one of the small naval vessels the English government maintained in the Caribbean, but the description would be just as accurate for many small steam vessels of the period.

With the conquest of the oceans, the early adventures of steam-powered vessels came to an end. In the future lay the luxury ships with their beautifully decorated interiors and the atmosphere of grand hotels. Gigantic steamships were built, such as the 692-foot-long *Great Eastern* and floating cities such as the *Queen Elizabeth* of one thousand and thirty-one feet. In the 1900s such vessels as the *Queen Elizabeth* went to sea with jewelry stores, beauty parlors, swimming pools, and theaters aboard. Even river steamboats were soon to become: "Like moving mountains of light and flame, so brilliantly are these enormous leviathans illuminated outside and inside."

As John Fitch had said about steam navigation in 1792: "This, sir, will be the method of crossing the Atlantic, whether I bring it to perfection or not." These later vessels were a far cry from Fitch's *Experiment*, or Stevens's *Phoenix*, yet in such early steamboats the idea of steam navigation was tested and found practical. A power independent of wind, tide, and current had been put to work, a revolution in engineering had taken place, and a new era in transportation had begun.

Bibliography

Adams, J. T. *Dictionary of American History*. Charles Scribner's Sons, 1940.

Albion, R. G. *The Rise of New York Port: 1815–1860*. With the collaboration of J. B. Pope. Charles Scribner's Sons, 1939.

Allen, W., Editor. *Transatlantic Crossing*. William Morrow & Co., Inc., 1971.

American and Commercial Daily Advertiser. Baltimore, August 20, 24, and 25, 1807.

Andrist, R. K., Editor. *Making of a Nation*. American Heritage Publishing Co., Inc., 1968.

Babcock, F. L. *Spanning the Atlantic*. Alfred A. Knopf, 1931.

Baker, W. A., and Tryckare, T. *The Engine Powered Vessel*. Grosset & Dunlap, 1965.

Baltimore, Vol. XVI, No. 1, "Steam Sloop *Albermarle*." Baltimore, October 1923.

Bathe, B. W. *Steamships–Merchant Ships to 1880*. Her Majesty's Stationery Office, 1962.

Bellington, R. A., and Ridge, M., Editors. *America's Frontier Story*. Holt, Rinehart & Winston, 1969.

Bernstein, H. T. *Steamboats on the Ganges*. Orient Longmans Publishing Co., 1960.

Billigmeier, R. H., and Picard, F. A., Editors. *The Old Land and the New: The Journals of Two Swiss Families in America in the 1820's*. University of Minnesota Press, 1965.

Blake, G. *British Ships and Shipbuilding*. Colins, 1946.

Blake, N. M. *A History of American Life and Thought*. McGraw-Hill Book Co., Inc., 1963.

Boorstin, D. J. *The Americans: The National Experience*. Random House, 1965.

Boyd, T. *Poor John Fitch—Inventor of the Steamboat*. G. P. Putnam's Sons, 1935.

Braynard, F. O. *S. S. Savannah*. University of Georgia Press, 1963.

Briggs, A. *The Nineteenth Century*. Thames & Hudson, 1970.

Brown, Alexander Crosby. *The Sheet Iron Steamboat Codorus*. Museum Publication No. 21, The Mariners' Museum, 1950.

————. *Twin Ships: Notes on the Chronological History of the Use of Multiple Hulled Vessels.* Museum Publication No. 5, The Mariners' Museum, 1939.

Brown, R., and Brown, M., Editors. *Impressions of America.* Harcourt, Brace & World, Inc., 1966.

Brown, R. H. *Historical Geography of the United States.* Harcourt, Brace & World, Inc., 1948.

Buchanan, L. *Ships of Steam.* McGraw-Hill Book Co., Inc., 1956.

Burgess, R. H., and Wood, H. G. *Steamboats out of Baltimore.* Tidewater Publishers, 1968.

Chamber's Journal of Popular Literature, Science & Art, Vol. 12, No. 596. "Jonathan Hulls." London and Edinburgh, 1875.

Chapelle, H. I. *The National Watercraft Collection.* U.S. National Museum Bulletin 219, Smithsonian Institution, 1960.

————. *The Pioneer Steamship Savannah: A Study for a Scale Model.* Smithsonian Institution, 1961.

Clark, W. H. *Railroads & Rivers: The Story of Inland Transportation.* L. C. Page & Co., 1939.

Commager, H. S., Editor. *Documents of American History.* 8th Edition. Appleton-Century-Crofts, 1968.

Cowie, J. S. *Mines, Minelayers and Minelaying.* Oxford University Press, 1949.

Cutler, C. C. *Queens of the Western Ocean.* United States Naval Institute, 1961.

Dayton, F. E. *Steamboat Days.* Originally published by Frederick A. Stokes Co., 1925; reprinted by Tudor Publishing Co., 1939.

Dean, F. E. *Famous River Craft of the World.* Frederick Muller Ltd., 1959.

Dickinson, H. W. *Robert Fulton.* The Bodley Head, 1913.

Donovan, F. R. *River Boats of America.* Thomas Y. Crowell Co., 1966.

Dorsey, F. L. *Master of the Mississippi: Henry Shreve.* Houghton Mifflin Co., 1941.

Drachmann, A. G. *The Mechanical Technology of Greek and Roman Antiquity.* The University of Wisconsin Press, 1963.

Drago, H. S. *The Steamboaters.* Dodd, Mead & Co., 1967.

Dunbar, S. *A History of Travel in America.* Originally published by Yale University Press, 1914; reprinted by Tudor Publishing Co., 1937.

Durant, J., and Durant, A. *Pictorial History of American Ships.* A. S. Barnes and Co., 1953.

Durant, W., and Durant, A. *Rousseau and Revolution: 1715–1789.* Simon & Schuster, 1967.

Earl, A. M. *Stage-Coach and Tavern Days.* The Macmillan Co., 1900.

Emmerson, J. C. *The Steamboat Comes to Norfolk Harbor, and the Log of the First Ten Years.* Edwards Brothers, Inc., 1949.

Eskew, G. L. *The Pageant of the Packets: A Book of American Steamboating.* Henry Holt & Co., 1929.

Eskew, G. L., as told to A. C. Harding. *America Rides the Liners.* Coward-McCann, Inc., 1956.

Farbrother, R., Editor. *Ships: A Collection of Essays.* Paul Hamlyn, 1963.

Farr, G. *West Country Passenger Steamers.* Richard Tilling, 1956.

Fayle, C. E. *A Short History of the World's Shipping.* The Dial Press, 1933.

Flexner, J. T. *Steamboats Come True.* Viking Press, 1944.

Flint, T. *Recollections of the Last Ten Years in the Valley of the Mississippi.* Originally published by Cummings, Hilliard, and Co., 1826; unabridged republication, Da Capo Press, A Division of Plenum Publishing Corp., 1968.

Fogel, R. W. *Railroads and American Economic Growth: Essays in Econometric History.* Johns Hopkins Press, 1964.

Footner, H. *Rivers of the Eastern Shore.* Tidewater Publishers, 1944.

Gibbs, C. R. V. *Passenger Liners of the Western Ocean.* John De Graff, Inc., 1952.

Hall, J. *The West: Its Commerce and Navigation.* Originally published, 1848; reprinted by Burt Franklin, 1970.

Handlin, O., Editor. *This Was America.* Harper & Row, Publishers, 1949.

Havighurst, W. *Voices on the River.* The Macmillan Company, 1964.

Hill, R. N. *Sidewheeler Saga—A Chronicle of Steamboating.* Rinehart & Co., Inc., 1953.

Hulbert, A. B. *The Paths of Inland Commerce.* Yale University Press, 1920.

Hunter, L. C. *Steamboats on the Western Rivers: An Economic and Technological History.* Harvard University Press, 1949.

Hunt's Merchant Magazine, Freeman Hunt, Editor. Vol. XV, No. V. "Robert Fulton's First Voyage." November 1846.

Hyde, F. E. *Shipping Enterprise and Management: 1830–1939.* Liverpool University Press, 1967.

Jackson, G. G. *The Ship Under Steam.* Charles Scribner's Sons, 1928.

Kier, M. *Pageant of America,* Vol. 4. "The March of Commerce." Edited by R. H. Gabriel, Yale University Press, 1927.

Knox, T. W. *The Life of Robert Fulton & A History of Steam Navigation.* G. P. Putnam's Sons; originally published 1886, republished 1900.

Lacour-Gayet, R. *Everyday Life in the United States Before the Civil War: 1830–1860.* Translated by Mary Ilford. Frederick Ungar Publishing Co., 1969.

Langdon, W. C. *Everyday Things in American Life: 1776–1867.* Charles Scribner's Sons, 1941.

Lass, W. E. *A History of Steamboating on the Upper Missouri River.* University of Nebraska Press, 1962.

Latrobe, J. *The First Steamboat Voyage on the West-*

ern Waters. Maryland Historical Society Fund Publications Nos. 1–7, 1867–1877.

————. *A Lost Chapter in the History of the Steamboat.* Maryland Historical Society Fund Publications Nos. 1–7, 1867–1877.

Lee, N. E. *Travel & Transport Through the Ages.* Melbourne University Press, 1951.

Leslie, R. F. *The Age of Transformation.* Blandford Press, 1964.

Lindsay, J. *The Ancient World.* G. P. Putnam's, 1968.

Long, D. F., and Riegal, R. E. *The American Story,* Volume One: "Youth." McGraw-Hill Book Co., Inc., 1955.

MacCurdy, E. *The Notebooks of Leonardo da Vinci.* Jonathan Cape, 1938.

McDowell, W. *The Shape of Ships.* Roy Publishers, 1948.

McKay, R. C. *South Street: A Maritime History of New York.* Originally published 1934; reprinted 7 C's Press, Inc., 1969.

McQueen, J. *A General Plan for a Mail Communication by Steam.* London, no publisher listed, 1838.

Magazine of American History, Vol. XXVIII, No. 3. "Early American Steam Navigation." September 1892.

Malone, D., and Rauch, B. *The Republic Comes of Age: 1789–1841.* Appleton-Century-Crofts, 1960.

Marder, A. J., Editor. *Fear God and Dread Nought: The Correspondence of Admiral of the Fleet Lord Fisher of Kilverstone.* Jonathan Cape, 1952.

Marryat, F. *A Diary in America.* Originally published 1839, edited by S. Jackman; reprinted Alfred A. Knopf, 1962.

Maryland Gazette, Annapolis. Thursday, July 30, 1807, Mr. Fulton's experiment in blowing up ships; Thursday, July 21, 1808, excerpt from the Hudson, N.Y., *Hudson Bee* on the enlarged *Clermont;* August 4, 1808, *The Washington National Intelligencer* story on the *Clermont;* January 31, 1810, *Raritan* sunk.

Melville, H. *Journal of a Visit to London.* Harvard University Press, 1948.

Merchant Magazine and Commercial Review, Vol. 17. "Lake Ontario Steam Navigation," 1847.

Niles' Weekly Register. Editor, H. Niles. Baltimore. May 21, 1814; July 9, 1814; September 3, 1815; July 6, 1816; July 20, 1816; October 19, 1816; March 15, 1817; May 17, 1817; August 30, 1817; September 19, 1817.

North American Review, Vol. L, No. CVI. "Steamboat Disasters." Boston, January 1840.

Olmsted, F. L. *The Cotton Kingdom.* 2 vols. Originally published by Mason Brothers, 1861; reprinted with an introduction by Arthur M. Schlesinger, Alfred A. Knopf, 1966.

Perry, J. *American Ferryboats.* Wilfred Funk, Inc., 1957.

Peterson, W. J. *Steamboating on the Upper Mississippi.* The State Historical Society of Iowa, 1968.

Phillips-Birt, D. *When Luxury Went to Sea.* St. Martin's Press, 1971.

Port Folio, edited by J. E. Hall. Vol. XIX, 1825.

Potter's American Monthly Magazine. "Early Steamboat Navigation." Vol. IV, No. 39. March 1875.

Quick, H., and Quick, E. *Mississippi Steamboatin'— A History of Steamboating on the Mississippi and Its Tributaries.* Henry Holt, 1926.

Rolt, L. T. C. *Thomas Newcomen—The Prehistory of the Steam Engine.* David and Charles Davlish Macdonald, 1963.

Rowland, K. T. *Steam at Sea.* Praeger Publishers, 1970.

Sanford, C. L., Editor. *Quest for America—1810–1824, Documents in American Civilization.* New York University Press, 1964.

Schapiro, J. S. *Modern and Contemporary European History—1815–1952.* Houghton Mifflin Co., 1953.

Scientific American, Vol. LXXII, No. 25. "History of Early Steam Navigation." March 28, 1891, and December 21, 1895.

Sellers, G. E. *Early Engineering Reminiscences, 1815–1840.* Edited by E. S. Ferguson. Smithsonian Bulletin 238, 1965.

Sewell-Stevenson. *Dictionary of American Biography.* Edited by D. Malone. Charles Scribner's Sons, 1935.

Shannahan, J. H. K. *Steamboat'n Days.* The Norman Publishing House, 1930.

Sinclair, H. *The Port of New Orleans.* Doubleday, Doran & Co., Inc., 1942.

Sketches of History, Life, and Manners in the United States: by a Traveller. Printed for the Author, New Haven, 1826.

Stanton, S. W. *Great Lakes Steam Vessels.* Meriden Gravure Co., 1962.

Stevers, N. D., and Pendlebury, J. *Sealanes: Man's Conquest of the Ocean.* Milton, Balch and Co., 1935.

Storer, J. D. *A Simple History of the Steam Engine.* John Baker Publishers, 1969.

Thorne, O. O., Editor. *Chamber's Biographical Dictionary.* St. Martin's press reprint of 1897 original, 1969.

Thurston, R. H. *A History of the Growth of the Steam Engine.* Originally published by Cornell University Press, 1878; reprinted by Cornell University Press, 1939.

Tryon, W. S., Editor. *Mirror for Americans—1790–1870.* The University of Chicago Press, 1952.

Turner, F. J. *The Frontier in American History.* Henry Holt & Co.; originally published 1920; reprinted in revised editions, 1947 and 1958.

Tute, W. *Atlantic Conquest.* Little, Brown and Co., 1962.

Tyler, D. B. *Steam Conquers the Atlantic.* Appleton-Century Co., Inc., 1939.

Whitlark, F. L. *Introduction to the Lakes.* Greenwich Book Publishing Co., 1959.

Wilson, Mitchell. *American Science and Invention: A Pictorial History.* Simon & Schuster, 1954.

Wolfe, R. *Yankee Ships.* The Bobbs-Merrill Co., Inc., 1953.

Index